Bullseye!

Yasutaka Tsutsui

Bullseye!
by Yasutaka Tsutsui
Copyright © 2017 Yasutaka Tsutsui

Additional copyright information on page 221.

This English translation arranged through Andrew Nurnberg Associates, London.

Translation copyright © 2017 Andrew Driver

FG-JP0052L
ISBN: 978-4-902075-86-1

Edited by Nancy H. Ross
Cover by Youchan Ito, Togoru Co., Ltd.

Kurodahan Press
KURODAHAN.COM

Bullseye!

Yasutaka Tsutsui

Translated By

Andrew Driver

Contents

Introduction

Yasutaka Tsutsui: A Deconstructor of Reality

Comic storyteller, novelist, playwright, science fiction writer, actor, TV personality, nonconformist, guru of metafiction, jazz musician — seems it's hard to pin a label on Yasutaka Tsutsui. Born in 1934, he studied aesthetics and art at Doshisha University in Kyoto and always aspired to be an actor. But somehow he ended up being a writer.

In 1960, Tsutsui started the science fiction fanzine *NULL* with his brothers, and he's been deconstructing reality ever since. He published his first collection of short stories, *Tokaido Sensō* (The Tokaido War), in 1965. It was followed closely by his first novel, *48 Oku no Mōsō* (4.8 Billion Delusions) later that year. Over the next five decades, he went on to produce dozens of novels and hundreds of short stories in genres ranging from dark comedy to science fiction and surrealism. He has collected a number of literary prizes along the way; in 1997, he was named a Chevalier of the Order of Arts and Letters by the French government.

But the Naoki Prize, Japan's most coveted literary award, has eluded him, despite several nominations. Why might that be? Perhaps it's because people aren't quite sure what to make of Tsutsui. He doesn't exactly play by the rules, after all. Is he "serious?" Or is he "popular?" He has certainly done much to blur the boundaries between the two. He spurns political correctness; he smokes heavily against his doctor's advice. In short, he's a bit of a rebel.

Tsutsui has continually sought new ways to defy description, questioning the purpose of literature and the relevance of social values. "To me, science fiction is just another way of deconstructing reality, just as surrealism was," he said in a 1997 interview (Dalkey Archive Press, 2002). "Of course I could have employed other approaches. For example, I could have become a painter, if only I had had the talent. Writing was the only way left for me to deconstruct reality. When I was at university, I wanted to become a comic actor. That seemed to be another way to deconstruct reality. Comedy was a very important medium for me."

Bullseye! is the second collection of Tsutsui short stories to appear in English translation, after *Salmonella Men on Planet Porno* (Alma Books, 2006). But while for that publication I mainly gathered stories from a single Japanese collection, *Ore ni Kansuru Uwasa* (Rumours about Me), with a few judicious additions, *Bullseye!* is more like a journey through Tsutsui's long career as one of Japan's best-known authors. The journey is of course not linear but meanders through the ages like one of Tsutsui's deluded antiheroes. We have "Zarathustra on Mars" from 1973. Fast forward to "Having a Laugh" from 2015, then back to 1973 for "The Good Old Days." We meet Tsutsui as a younger man, writing of office workers and their foibles, sex robots, future life on distant planets, squabbling families, the loss of loved ones — virtually every aspect of human frailty, in fact. We meet him again in older age, even appearing as himself in the later stories — so much so that, as we reach the end of his journey, we cannot be sure that he is not just writing about himself.

The title story "Bullseye!" comes from Tsutsui's latest and probably last collection in Japanese, *Sekai wa Gojōdan*, the title story of which appears here as "Having a Laugh." It shows Tsutsui in full satirical flow, railing surreally against social absurdity as only he knows how, but with a crucial twist: his first-person protagonist is neither a dreary salaried worker nor a henpecked husband, but one of Japan's "super-aged" — confused, mocked, and ultimately dangerous.

Bullseye! highlights an important shift in Tsutsui's subject matter since his early forays into metafiction. "You're too obsessed with death these days," says the cantankerous old watchmaker in "The Countdown Clock" — death, old age, disease and senility, to be exact. More of the stories toward the end of this collection are concerned with these themes, and, unsurprisingly, more of them are from recent works.

Tsutsui has already declared his novel-writing days over, and he told me that, barring the occasional magazine submission, time may be up on his short stories as well. "The ideas aren't coming any more," he said with blunt honesty. We can only hope that more of his existing works will find their way to a wider audience in the fullness of time.

My thanks to Kurodahan Press for making this publication possible.

Andrew Driver
June 2017

Bullseye!

THERE WAS A CLOCK on the dining room table. It worshipped me. Clocks are funny things, but a clock worshipping a person is simply ridiculous.

The clock asked me to smash my coffee cup on the floor, so that's what I did.

I'd just been thinking how it wasn't *me* that was *expanding* but the *universe* that was actually *shrinking*, and was about to resume this train of thought when a woman came out of the kitchen.

"What happened?" she asked in that condescending manner.

I said nothing but just kept my mind on the Goddess of Folly and *The Ship of Fools*. Eventually, the woman noticed the broken cup on the floor. "Oh no," she groaned.

She went back into the kitchen, where I assumed she'd pour me another coffee. But no, out she came with a brush and dustpan and started clearing up the mess. That really made me mad. Not the kind of mad that makes you shout and scream, lash out wildly, kill someone or ejaculate. No – I just got up in silence.

The woman gave me a wide-eyed look as if to say, *Whatever will he do next?*

"Go on then," I said. "Give me that wide-eyed look, like you don't know what the senile old fool's going to do next. You think I'm demented, but I'm not. What I've got is *paraphrasia*, otherwise known as *compatibilitis*."

It must have been some time later, for I was back in my room. Time has been jumping about and getting shorter recently, so I tend to forget things. This is probably a leap of logic. But that's OK, as it's good for developing powers of thought.

I heard voices coming from the living room.

"Kenji will be here at five," the woman was saying. "Make sure you give it to him. You know? The two million we got from the bank. He'll be in a real fix if he doesn't get it today."

"Why didn't you just do a bank transfer?" said a man with a stupid-sounding voice. I couldn't remember hearing such a stupid-sounding voice in the house before.

"Are you crazy? If I'd transferred it, they'd be able to trace who sent it!"

"OK, OK. It's in the bank envelope, right?"

"Right. You're working from home today, yes? You'll be at home?"

"Yeah, yeah. Sure."

The woman seemed to leave the house at that point, so I thought I'd better be on my way too. I had to give a lecture at the university that afternoon. I teach rhetorical density, and of course my explanation has to be based on iconographic interpretation. I took a suit out of my wardrobe and put it on. Well, I couldn't have gone out in my pajamas, could I now? I would only have been picked up and carted back like some "aged wanderer".

The obvious thing was to wear a shirt and tie as well, but another obvious thing was that I could have strangled myself by tying the tie too tight. In other words, it was as obvious as the fact that epistemological realism and the anaphoric theory of truth are just empty mutterings worthy of no scrutiny at all. Students are all gullible fools, but, there again, they wouldn't be students if they weren't gullible.

I went back to the living room in an "early afternoon" kind of mood. The bank envelope was lying on the table. Now it goes without saying that two million yen in cash is just asking to be stolen. And as I was the only person there to steal it, I slipped it into my pocket and went to the front door, based on the exegetical understanding that I would take the money with me. I could hear the monotonous clackety-clack of a computer keyboard coming

2

from the study at the back and a voice saying, "Mind how you go." Huh. He was only fishing to see where I was off to.

I stepped out onto a typical residential street when time suddenly jumped again. Now I was walking through a park. It seemed familiar, but, then again, it didn't. I was going to give a *talk* but ended up in a *park*, so it was a kind of analogical leap. Hello! I seem to have acquired montage skills. Sunlight poured down, along with hailstones; gusts of wind flitted across, then made their excuses and left. I saw a building that looked like a police box near the park entrance, so I walked over to it. Sitting at the desk was a brazenfaced young officer, blissfully unaware that he would one day be killed.

"Excuse me, I wonder if you could help me," I said, doing my best to sound like Orson Welles in *The Third Man*.

"Certainly, sir. What seems to be the problem?" The officer stood up, startled perhaps by my voice and appearance.

"I'm supposed to be giving a lecture, but I've forgotten where it is."

"Oh dear, sir. That won't do."

"It certainly won't. After all, it's the world's first public lecture on the automaticity of repetition in the energy of desire. At Bridgestone University. It must be somewhere near here."

"Bridgestone, sir? I haven't heard of that one. Just a minute."

He took a cursory glance at a map on the wall before calling out to a colleague in the back room.

"Hey, is there a Bridgestone University round here?" he said as he went through.

What an idiot – an idiot of the very highest order. He'd left his pistol on the desk. Now, it goes without saying that a pistol lying on a desk is just asking to be stolen. And as I was the only person there to steal it, I slipped it out of its holster, wedged it under my belt and walked out. The street outside was a scene of utter chaotic madness, enough to make you scream at the nonsensical nature of human existence, such as you'd find at about two in the afternoon.

But oh! What a vermin-infested ruin of a society it was out

3

there. The hell of contemporary Japan – a writhing, squirming, festering cesspit of humanity, where the billowing waves of the floating world swallow up people like so much garbage, making no distinction between good or evil, cunning or naive, then spew them out again and leave them there to rot. Still, I didn't let that bother me; I just carried on walking in compliance with the Road Traffic Act.

The sun had started to set and I was beginning to feel tired, so I took a seat at a streetside café and started to take the pistol apart. I must have been a policeman in the past, or perhaps an officer in the Self-Defence Forces. I might even have been a lieutenant in the old Imperial Army, for I could have dismantled and reassembled that gun with my eyes closed.

"Hey, what a totally realistic toy," the waiter's vacuous smile seemed to say as he plonked a glass of water on my table.

"I'll have a café latte chocolat," I said, "and some bullets for a 22-caliber revolver."

"Not a problem, sir. One café latte chocolat. Sorry, we don't do bullets."

OK, OK. I counted the bullets in the cylinder. Six. That meant I could kill six people, which would have to do for now. After re-assembling the gun I took the bank envelope out of my pocket and started counting the bundles of ten-thousand yen notes. When I got to the first million I accidentally started counting millions instead of ten-thousands, so I had to go back to the beginning and start all over again. It took a while, but in the end I counted – yes! – exactly two million yen.

The other customers were looking at me goggle-eyed by now. A man sitting near me was talking too loud on his mobile, so I smashed my glass on the sidewalk and gave him a murderous stare. He merely cast a dubious look in my direction then went straight back to jabbering on about how it was the budget, how it was the government, how it was the former Director of the Economic Planning Agency, how those people don't know what they're doing anyway, jabber jabber jabber jabber jabber jabber. So this time I hurled my cup of café latte chocolat hard at the sidewalk. If that didn't stop him, I was prepared to smash my chair over his head, but now, at last, he obediently folded away his mobile with a look of terror on his face.

The waiter came out, so I gave him a ten-thousand yen note and got up to go. As I turned to leave, I commented that the café's socioeconomic space should be taken apart and rebuilt but that he could keep the change as a tip.

"Quite right, sir. Thank you, sir," he called out behind me.

A group of four youths had been watching from the roadside while I counted the money. As soon as I left the café, they darted into the shade of a building, presumably intent on robbing me. I wondered what I could do to make their task easier, and decided to turn off the main road into a little shopping street. From there, I stepped into a side alley that was so narrow it could only be entered sideways – well, not quite that narrow, but you get the drift. The alley was lined with bars, but, luckily, they hadn't opened yet; the only other living things in the alley were rats.

"Hey. Old man."

Ah! Welcome, boys! I turned to face them with a grin, anticipating the pleasure of killing them. The youth at the front was an ugly version of Big G from Doraemon. The other three were a young Alec Guinness, a Buddhist stupa with a face drawn in marker pen, and a ceramic raccoon dog about to collapse in a heap.

"What's the joke, old man? Just give us the money," snapped Big G, obviously the ringleader.

"The French avant garde poet and surrealist Gherasim Luca wrote this poem," I said, and started to recite.

je t'aime
passionnément aimante je
t'aime je t'aime passionnément
je t'ai je t'aime passionné né
je t'aime passionné
je t'aime passionnément je t'aime
je t'aime passio passionnément . . .

"What's he on about?"

"Old man's gone gaga!"

"It's his medication, ennit!"

The youths looked at each other and started laughing.

"Shut up and listen!" I shouted. "This is what you want, isn't it?"

I took the envelope out of my pocket and shook it at them. The laughter stopped instantly, replaced by a look of desperate longing in their glazed eyes, as if they'd just found a bottle of Coke in a desert.

"Boys, let me tell you a story. One day, a young man went to Gherasim Luca and asked him to read a poem he had written. Luca took out a gun and said, 'OK, I'll read it, but if you're not a *real* writer, I'm going to shoot you.' And then he read the poem."

As I spoke, I took the pistol from my belt. "Of course, the poem was lousy, so he shot the young man. Now here's what I want you to do: I want you to recite a poem. Anything you like. Something beautiful like the one just now. OK, it doesn't have to be a poem, it could be a song, a haiku, a limerick, or just doggerel. If it moves me, I'll give you the money. If not, you're history."

Big G appeared stunned for a moment then burst into laughter. "Yeah, right! With a toy gun!" And he tried to snatch it from my hand.

So I fired. The recoil made the barrel jump upward. A window in a nearby building shattered. I lurched back a step or two in surprise, then staggered around for a few more steps before regaining my composure. Did that always happen with guns? I thought I must be getting senile. I looked around; three of the youths had run for their lives, and only the ceramic raccoon dog remained. He had stumbled over a bin and now lay pathetically sprawled at the side of the alley. I went up to him and held the muzzle of the gun to his temple.

"How does it feel to be ending your short miserable life in a godforsaken back alley surrounded by the stink of urine?"

"Uh, I just peed myself," said the ceramic raccoon dog. With that, his eyes rolled up into his head and he fainted. His trousers were soaked, and now they stank of urine too.

Shooting an unconscious person would have been no fun at all, so I left him there and walked away.

Actually, I regretted wasting the first bullet as it was; the remaining five were now as precious as the few hairs left on a balding man's head. I thought of firing into the shopping street, but it was too busy to get a good shot, and, anyway, the people there were just too ordinary. Shooting them would have been pointless. I needed to find a higher grade of target, someone really worth shooting. So I made my way to the station plaza – decidedly more upmarket and full of people who were really crying out to be shot.

As I wandered around in search of my prey, I spotted a poster on a public noticeboard. It announced that a lecture on *The Tale of Genji* was to be held in the Community Center later that afternoon; the speaker was a professor I'd never heard of, from a university I'd never heard of. Community Center . . . Hmm . . . Targets were sure to be lined up like ducks in a shooting gallery there!

The Community Center was right next to the noticeboard. I ignored the front door and went in through the staff entrance at the side. The entrance led to a waiting room, which was deserted but for six chairs set around a table as if they were having a meeting.

From the adjacent hall, I could hear someone talking over a microphone. I opened the door and passed through the darkened wings toward the stage, where a man with a swindler's smile was addressing the audience. He looked like a city employee and seemed to be introducing the guest speaker. A plump middle-aged man wearing a neat suit, presumably the speaker, was sitting in the dim light of the wings stage left, waiting for his turn to appear. I slipped the pistol out of my belt and brought the butt down on his thinning pate from behind. He neither cried out nor groaned but meekly fell unconscious. I dragged his heavy body behind the drape of a black stage curtain and left him lying there like an octopus sprawled on the ocean floor.

"So, over to you, Professor."

The man with the swindler's smile started to clap, urging the audience to do the same, then withdrew to the wings stage right. I stepped out onto the brightly lit podium and strode up to the lectern; it was a sturdy lectern with a vase of flowers perched precariously on one side. Looking out over the audience, I saw row upon row of graying heads, goofy teeth, metal-framed spectacles, plump middles, tree-trunk legs, midgets, shriveled toads, cheap necklaces, thickly daubed lipstick, bleached hair, purple-dyed fringes, gums exposed even when not smiling. . . . And most of them belonged to women. I saw a couple sitting in the front row. The wife was of course a woman, but the husband was also a woman. Behind them was another woman with her three children. One of them was a girl, and, of course, the other two were also girls. I had half expected it, but now I realized that, goodness me, they were all women.

I started to talk nonetheless. I had a vague memory of giving lectures on *The Tale of Genji* in my time as a university professor, and, although that memory was rapidly dimming, I was sure I could muddle through.

"Good afternoon. I've just turned up here today, but I think I can muddle through. Yes. I'm sure I can muddle through, so please don't worry. So, on to the theme of my talk, *The Tale of Genji*. Actually, there's no such thing as *The Tale of Genji*. That's because it originally had no title; books tended not to have titles back then. So what did people call it? They could have called it *Carry on Genji!* or maybe *Confessions of a Saucy Courtier*. Nevertheless it seems there really was a person called Murasaki Shikibu, though it's not clear whether she actually was the author. What's certain is that the work was well known and highly regarded in its day. Murasaki is said to have completed it while in the service of Fujiwara no Shoshi, second consort to the Emperor Ichijo, but it's hard to believe she could have produced such a massive volume on her own. She must have been assisted in no small measure by people like her patron Fujiwara no Michinaga.

"Now it's not just me saying that. Even scholars who claim Murasaki wrote it all still admit that Michinaga must have had a hand in it. Some people say Murasaki's daughter Daini no Sanmi must have been asked to write some of it, or that her supposedly deceased father Fujiwara no Tametoki or even her definitely deceased husband Fujiwara no Nobutaka was brought back from the other side by a spiritual medium to write it. Now on to the work itself. Well, it's trash. A failed epic indeed. Why? Well, just look at it: protagonist keeps changing, story jumps all over the place, style is inconsistent. It even finishes in the middle of a sentence. As for the plot, after the protagonist dies, we have an endless series of episodes going on and on like goldfish shit, storyline topsy-turvy, inconsistent, right up to the grandson's generation. To me, the reason for this is clear: because the work was so highly regarded, local women were fascinated and thought they would try writing some episodes themselves. So they took their efforts to the court to show Murasaki. And no doubt Murasaki made a few judicious alterations before putting them all together as the infamous *Uji Chapters*.

"And what are *they* all about? There's a limit to taking the piss, you know. Stop taking the piss, will you? Ah, sorry. Got a bit carried away there. So why is this work still so highly regarded today? And why does every single contemporary translation fly off the shelves time and time again? It's because the readers are all fools. And who are those readers? All you foolish women, of course, who don't get the point of artistic license. Encouraged by female academics who imagine they see feminist ideas in this book, connotations of an Eros-like dimension have assumed social currency amid the rampant eroticism not just of this town but of every other one too. A bond of sorority based on vaginal thinking arises just because the author was a woman, so that even today we have gatherings of vaginal thinkers summoned by the collective subconscious, like this one. The problem here is the desire or *non-desire* present in the act of reading, and in particular the social forces that transform reading into a moral duty, as with this work. And it is all of you, all of you who have flocked here like seagulls, guided only by the almost ritualistic vestiges of vaginal thinking by foolish women. 'Have you read it? –Ooh yes! I've read it! Have *you* read it? –Ooh yes! I've read it too. –Ooh! –Ooh!' And where will it all end? You may well ask. All I can say is it will surely end in hell."

As I spoke, I was growing increasingly annoyed with the vase on the lectern. The vase was purple and full of yellow flowers, probably chrysanthemums, and kept singing things like *The toilet's next door*. Now that was enough to get on anyone's nerves, so I stretched out my right arm and batted the vase away. It flew off to the right and shattered into pieces, scattering purple and yellow debris all over the podium.

A sudden movement in the wings caught my eye. Three or four men who looked like city employees were waiting to grab me, no doubt upset by my scathing rhetoric and my harsh treatment of the vase. I looked to the wings stage left and saw another two men there.

"What a load of rubbish!" exclaimed a woman in the front row, a studious type who'd been taking notes from the beginning. With that, she got up angrily and stomped off down the central aisle toward the main exit.

That triggered a mass exodus, as the women who'd been watching me impassively until then started a mad rush for the doors, babbling to each other as they went.

"Who on earth is he?"

"Some kind of madman!"

"Can't they stop him?"

I took the pistol out of my belt and aimed it at the audience. "Silence!" I shouted at the top of my voice. "Be quiet, all of you!"

Several women in the front row screamed.

"He's got a gun!"

"A gun!"

I laughed. "I see. This looks like a gun, does it? Yes, I'm sure it looks like a gun to you. But don't be fooled by appearances. This is, in fact, a *gun*."

And I fired. The recoil made the barrel jump upward. The bullet hit a spotlight in the ceiling, sending shards of glass showering down near the front row of the audience. Those who weren't already on their feet jumped up and tried to escape, accompanied by a chorus of shrieks and what sounded like yodeling. But the aisles were too narrow, and the only possible exits were three exceedingly tiny doors.

"Outta my way, ghouls!" I bellowed as I leapt down from the podium and charged toward the central aisle; that was my only hope, as those city employees were waiting for me in the wings. So I started hustling my way through the throng of women to reach the exit, pushing past fat backsides of all varieties, some flabby, some taut, some floppy, some pert. Glancing to my side, I noticed that even the original speaker, the one I'd knocked out, was trying to push his way through the women toward the exit.

"Hang on, what are you escaping for?" I asked.

"Because I'm ashamed," he replied, smiling apologetically. "Me, a university professor! Yet I was so nervous before going on that I actually fainted. It almost felt like, uh, something hit me, you know? And I still have this splitting headache. It's all so embarrassing. The only thing left for me is to run away. Was it you who stood in for me? Did you really say all those things, or was I dreaming? It was like you were expressing my innermost thoughts. I can't thank you enough."

We finally cleft a path through the mob of women and made our escape from the Community Center.

"So long," I said as we high-fived then went our separate ways. I trotted away from the station plaza, carried along by a litany of verbal invective and pointing fingers from the women who still lingered menacingly by the roadside. Afterwards, I realized I'd missed a great opportunity to fire off a few more shots. In fact, no one had been shot at all, which was most regrettable but couldn't be helped; I had been too busy chatting and escaping.

As I ran, I collided with an old woman who was walking toward me in what seemed to be a state of rigor mortis. She screeched loudly, which merely made me run faster.

"You shouldn't have left it on the table!"

"You should have picked it up! Dad must have taken it. What did Kenji say?"

Yasutaka Tsutsui

"He came at five on the dot but was pissed off when he realized the money wasn't there."

"He'll be in trouble at work now. Where on earth could Dad have gone?"

"Let's call the police and start a search."

"Are you crazy? If they find him, they'll find the money! And if they find the money, they'll ask him where he got it!"

"So we just wait till he comes home, right? I suppose he always does, after all. By the next day at least."

"I bet he's wrecking things all over the place again. And we have to cough up every time. We can only pray he comes back with all the money."

It was as if all my prayers had been answered, for as night fell I found myself in the busy entertainment district of Kabuki-cho in Shinjuku. I had enjoyed a hearty meal of shark's fin soup, sweet-and-sour pork and seafood fried rice in a Chinese restaurant where everyone was Chinese, including the customers, and now I was wandering amid the heaving mass of humanity, still searching for my prey. It seemed as if upright people, like me, never came near this place because it was full of devious people, like me. And there were touts and pimps everywhere. As soon as they saw someone dressed properly, like me, they would sidle up to them and mumble something about an experience that was out of this world, which I presumed to be the experience of dying.

"Sir, won't you step inside?" said a girl dressed like a flower seller as she handed me a card. She was cute, which was unusual in those parts.

"My, you are pretty. So very pretty. So pretty I could hug you, hold you close, squeeze you tight, ejaculate and finally strangle you to death."

"Ahahahahaha! You're so funny, sir!"

Judging from her asinine laugh, she was not particularly bright, but that was exactly the type I liked.

"So won't you step inside, sir?" she asked again.

"Will you join me if I do?"

"Ah . . . Why yes, sir!"

12

"In that case, let's step inside!"

The girl led me to the side of a building, up two dimly lit flights of stairs that smelt of stale urine, and through a hellish black stage door to a bar called *Dogma*. I briefly surveyed the premises before describing the scene.

"Well, what have we here? Nothing but four sofas occupied by three dumpy-looking girls and me as their only customer. The girls are a red-nosed reindeer, the comedian Akira Kishii, and Don Gabacho without a moustache. Behind the counter stands a slim bartender with a sharp look in his eye. There are no bottles lined up behind him, and there is dust on the corners of the counter. In other words, this is clearly and without a shadow of doubt a *clip joint*."

"Excuse me," interrupted the bartender, scowling at me darkly. "I'd ask you not to slag us off in public like that. Clip joint? On what basis?"

"Read two more pages and you'll find out." I put my arm around the flower seller's waist. "This one says she'll join me. Hope that's OK?"

The bartender pulled a sour face. He was obviously the owner as well. "She's supposed to be pulling in customers. But OK. Yuki, you can stay with sir." I guessed he had as many customers as he needed right now.

"Do you call all your customers 'sir'? I'm not a sir, though I may have been in the past," I said as I snuggled up to Yuki on one of the sofas – whereupon the other three girls gathered around us with expectations of easy profit written all over their faces.

"Got no half-decent liquor? Whiskey will do. You lot can drink what you like. But, anyway, that's a good name for a bar, *Dogma*. I once wrote a 2,650-page book costing 2,650 yen on the subject of dogmatic assertion, i.e. the prolegomena to the subconscious, arguing that, when discussing *langage* aimed at *langage* itself, *langage* is a metaphorical process of the *langage* of *langage*, as it were. In other words, the puzzled looks on your faces show that you are troubled to hear such incoherent rhetoric from one who cannot distinguish between theatrical discussion and the reality that this is a clip joint, and whose participation in the spectacle of your clip joint seems so very inconceivable. Has anyone here been raped?"

"Three guys," said Don Gabacho without a moustache.

"Gang rape, was it?"

"It was me that did it."

"Anyway, my book had two themes. One was the pain I felt from the delusion that my mother was having it off with me, the other was pleasure at the delusion that my mother was yanking me off. This is masturbation by the hand of another in the relationship between penis and penis, and the relationship between desire and the vagina on the theme of the delusion that the maid wanted to burn my penis with an iron. These were my two themes, but in the book I made a metaphorical connection between these and the subject. Be quiet!"

I picked up the bottle of Johnnie Walker Black Label from the table and smashed it on the floor. "*Decommission the reactor!*" I howled. "People keep screaming *Decommission the reactor!*"

The owner came over.

"Why did you break the bottle?"

"To shut them up! And these girls – they're not listening to a word I say! All they do is guzzle Morning Glory or whatever the hell it is. The only one who's laughing and paying any attention at all is Yuki. And that's only because I said some rude words."

"Well, what do you expect? Your subject matter is too difficult. It's boring." He started to clear the broken glass from the floor. "And this whiskey isn't cheap, you know."

"Oh, here we go! In that case, let's settle up now. How much do you want?" I said in the style of Jean Gabin in *Touchez pas au grisbi*. I took out the envelope, removed the wad of notes and slapped it down on the table.

The girls gasped. The owner stared at me with a sad look in his eyes. Yuki was the only one who seemed excited. "Ye-hey!" she gushed. "Sir's rich!"

"Excuse me," the owner said dolefully. "Why do you make fun of us like this? You don't think I enjoy my job, do you? I do it because I have no other option. The same goes for the girls. If I didn't employ them, they'd have nothing to live on."

As he spoke, his eyes grew moist with emotion. In fact, he was starting to look a bit like Peter Lorre, so I got to my feet, put a hand on his shoulder and tried to pacify him in a voice like my form teacher Mr Murakami from class 3B.

"It's all right, I understand. You mustn't cry. It's my fault. I should never have come to such a place, the lowest abyss in the whole of society. But, you know, all of us – you, me, and the girls too – we're all the same when it comes to bits in a computer. *Freeze!*"

I suddenly raised my voice, whipped the pistol out of my belt and jabbed it at the owner. "Don't start getting ideas now! What do you think this is, a Sunday school outing? Well it isn't. I'm going to rob you – just to put myself on your level, if you like. And you obviously won't be getting this lot." I put the two million back in my pocket. "So come on, hand over the dough!"

The girls pretended to be fairy princesses and screamed, while the owner scuttled off behind the bar as fast as a German cockroach. "What do you think you're doing?" he howled.

"Is it not clear yet? This is a robbery! You may of course call the police, but you will hand over all the money in the till first. And I won't pay my bill. Then the police will arrest me. And they all lived happy ever after."

"What the hell are you on about?" the owner yelled, almost screaming. "You're not right in the head!"

"There's nothing wrong with my head. This is a robbery. Call the police, quick. How many times must I say it? Huh, thick as pigshit. Right!" And I fired without warning.

The recoil made the barrel jump upward; the bullet smashed a bottle and a glass in the cabinet behind the bar. The owner hollered in terror as he ducked out of sight. Three of the girls fled to the corners of the room, ululating like female Tarzans. Only Yuki remained on the sofa, where she laughed and jigged up and down with glee.

"Got the idea now? So come on, pick up the phone."

"All right, all right! I will, I will!" The owner pulled out his mobile and pressed some numbers. "Police? I want to report a robbery. . . . Yes. It's a bar called *Dogma* on the third floor of the Bodhi Building on Central Street. . . . He's still inside. No, really. No, it's not just an argument. No, no, this isn't a clip joint. No, really, he just fired a gun. I tell you it's true!"

To help him along, I fired off a few shots at the cabinet behind the bar. Yuki shrieked in delight. The red-nosed reindeer crouched on the floor and covered her head with a cushion while chanting the Mantra of the Unfailing Rope Snare. Akira Kishii uttered what sounded like death throes, with legs spread wide and grubby red knickers in full view. Don Gabacho without a moustache made a dash for the door but collided with the wall instead, then turned and bawled her eyes out.

"Ow! Ow! Owww! Please stop! Or I won't have a face left!"

"So tell us where the old man's gone with the money!"

"I told you, he's gone gaga, you know, whatever it's called. He's not all there. Owww!"

"I don't give a shit about that! Where does he go? Don't say you don't know!"

"Uh . . . He sometimes goes round Kabuki-cho at night, but . . ."

"Kabuki-cho? If it's near Central Road, that's our patch, boss."

"Right. Kenji, you're coming with us. You know what he looks like."

I could hear police sirens wailing outside – at least two cars, maybe three. Time to go! The owner had fished out a collection of crumpled, dog-eared notes from various crevices and piled them together on the bar. A few thousand yen, I guessed. I gathered up the notes and stuffed them into my pockets, then thrust the barrel of the gun in the small of Yuki's back.

"This one's coming with me," I said melodramatically. "She'll be my hostage."

"Ye-hey! I'm a hostage, I'm a hostage!" Yuki was bouncing with excitement.

"Yuki," the owner pleaded with tears in his eyes. "Let's go see a movie some day."

I ignored him and took Yuki out to the stairwell. The gun was out of bullets, so I threw it onto the landing. From there, we continued down the stairs most amicably, like an odd couple out on a date. As we reached the bottom and stepped out into the street, we were met by a huddle of onlookers and two police cars with red lights rotating. I was expecting to be surrounded by officers and arrested right away, but nothing of the sort happened; instead, the cops remained hidden in the shadows, eyes and guns trained on the third-floor windows. Two officers ran up the stairs, passing us on the way. We might just as well have been invisible.

I went up to one of the police cars. An officer was crouched behind the open car door and staring up at the third floor of the building. "Excuse me, officer," I said. "This woman is a prostitute. She tried to proposition me. You must arrest her right away."

"Ye-hey! I'm a prostitute, I'm a prostitute!" Yuki squealed excitedly, then thought about it. "Ah, no. I'm not a prostitute, am I," she said with a sheepish look.

"Look, this isn't the time or place," the officer said irritably, his gaze still fixed on the third floor windows.

So I slipped off my belt and tied it around Yuki's neck. "In that case, I will punish this filthy whore myself. She's the kind of woman who breeds poisonous spiders in her belly and has badgers' faces peering out of her every soaking orifice! Why do you not arrest her? Now I know why they call the police *Dendrocacalia crepidifolia*!"

The officer turned to glare at me before hurriedly opening the back door of the car. "All right, get in. Both of you, get in the vehicle."

I removed the belt from Yuki's neck, then the two of us snuck straight into the comfy back seat of the police car. The officer went round to the driver's seat and picked up the radio receiver. "Yeah, Car Thirteen here. Got a weird old guy and a girl in my vehicle. Guy's probably senile and could harm the girl, so I'm taking them both in. Backup vehicle already here, so I'm returning to base, over."

"Roger, Car Thirteen. Mind how you go."

17

"Hey! There he is!"

"Where?!"

"There, in the police car! The old geezer sitting next to the girl. That's my dad!"

"You sure? Well, that's torn it. He's being taken in."

"We'll never get him out of there. Better forget it. Shit!"

The police seemed to think I was some kind of demented geriatric; they just didn't get it. They didn't ask my name or search me, but as it was getting late, they decided that I would spend a night in the cells and be questioned the next day. The thought of sharing a cell with Yuki made me feel like I was walking on water around Mont Saint Michel, but to my immense dismay, we were separated.

Alone, I passionately embraced a simple bed that welcomed me with a shake of its rickety legs before guiding me into a deep sleep. As day broke, I saw virtually the whole of Pasolini's *Oedipus Rex* unabridged in a dream. Some readers may be wondering why the police hadn't received a report about the stolen pistol, but the true reader is not concerned with such trivia. An officer came to ask if I needed anything to eat. I replied that I didn't want his stinking food, which didn't seem to please him much, so he took me straight to the interview room. The interview was a half-baked affair, with no one taking notes and only a single detective asking questions. The detective was a middle-aged man with a hangover; I amused myself by imagining the grotesque description Chandler would have given him. Sneering from the outset, his derisory smirk made his fleshy jowls look fleshier still.

"So, what's your name?" he asked.

"Tokugawa Ieyasu," I replied obligingly.

He leant forward as if to say *Just as I thought*. "And your date of birth?"

"January 31st, 1543."

"Please be serious."

"I am. Don't you know your history?"

The detective said nothing but languidly surveyed the ceiling for a moment. After a while, he turned back to me with a sneer. "What's three minus two?"

"Three minus two? The answers are infinite. Two minus one. One. One minus zero. A hundred minus ninety-nine. 16,328 minus 16,327 . . . No way is there just one answer, contrary to the delusions of your tiny mind. To be specific, there are infinitely numerous properties in systems of integers like Fermat's local field and the numbers derived from them. Even elementary number theory should be tackled without using fingers or toes. I am perfectly aware that you regard me as a demented geriatric, and I know my answer will only reinforce your view. This is the same as when Évariste Galois failed the entrance exam to the École Polytechnique because he felt the questions set by the examiners were too boring and so didn't answer them. Now let's move on to Gaussian integers. These could be seen as fundamental to the field of algebraic number theory, of which the Galois theory is a basic tool. Of course, that's true for other integers as well. Anyway, mathematics is the queen of sciences, as Victor Segaren said. I want to see Yuki. Immediately! Yuki! YUKI!"

Time jumped again. I don't know how many hours passed; maybe it was just minutes. I assumed it was some kind of literary omission or a spot of judicious editing, but I was still talking when I regained consciousness. That had never happened before. My conclusion was that mental activity must continue to develop as it leaps through inert space.

"This process of calculation, this algorithm, is troublesome because it requires too many cumulative thought processes each time. That's precisely why people invented computers; people do things heuristically, you see. It's like a quick and easy way of defecating without taking laxatives, otherwise known as the compendium method. When executed properly, the result is diarrhea."

The detective stood up, took out his mobile and started pacing aimlessly around the room as he spoke.

"Uh, Chief? Yeah. This guy we had in last night? I could do with some backup here. No no, it's just a bit much for me on my own. No, nothing like that. You'll know when you get here. Yeah."

He folded away his mobile and sighed before turning back to me. "I don't expect a straight answer from you, but . . ."

"But?"

"I'm busy. I've got a pile of cases on my hands, and I don't have time to waste on this interview. I need to finish it quickly, but you keep spouting all this incoherent crap."

He proceeded to moan about how hard police work was, how he was so overworked that his wife was going to divorce him, how this, how that, how the other. In fact, he only stopped when his superior stepped in. This was a somewhat younger but clearly brainier man who wore the spectacles of an intellectual. With him came a corpulent subordinate who resembled the sumo wrestler Takamisakari; maybe he was there to protect the chief. If I dared attack his boss with my stinging rhetoric and philosophical constructs, Takamisakari would step in, lift me up and hoist me out of the ring like a freshly caught prawn.

"What's the problem, Sudo? Want me to take over?"

"Yeah. Thanks, Chief." The fleshy-jowled detective stood up with a look of relief, vacated the seat opposite me and went to sit next to Takamisakari by the wall.

The chief, who was young enough to be my son, now resumed the questioning.

"So. First, please tell me your name."

"Shoichi Azumi," I replied with complete honesty. I even spelled it out for him.

The chief glared questioningly at Sudo, whose eyes now bulged until they were the size of hen's eggs.

"But just now he said it was Tokugawa Ieyasu!" Sudo protested.

"I would never say anything so ridiculous," I said calmly, with the quietly confident tone of a Tokyo University graduate. "Is there any record to prove I did?"

The chief glanced at the blank notepad on the desk. "No. There isn't."

Sudo leapt out of his chair in foaming contortions of apoplexy. "What's three minus two then? Answer me that!"

"The answer is *one*, of course," I said in a tone of still greater calm and self-control, like an inscrutable swordsmith from the feudal era, before turning back to the chief. "Your colleague has been harassing me with moronic questions like that ever since I came in. He's so overburdened with work that he wants to write me off as a demented old fool and get the case finished quickly, so he persists in asking ridiculous questions that cannot be answered, the intention being to confuse me. Then he can claim I wouldn't respond to questioning. Please take over from now on."

"Don't listen to him!" Sudo bellowed, face moistened by tears and perspiration. He squatted as if he were about to defecate and rudely jabbed a finger at me. "All he gave me was utter bull, not a single word of sense! He's just pretending to be normal now! Senile old fool's leading us by the nose! He's a complete nutter, I tell you!"

Takamisakari just managed to grab him from behind as he lunged at me.

The chief got up. "Sudo, a word outside please. Mr Azumi, if you would wait here."

"But Chief, Chief! It's a trick! Don't you see?" Sudo continued to wail as he left the room, more or less carried out by the chief and Takamisakari. The three then entered a heated debate just outside the door, before they finally took Sudo away and peace returned.

I took a pen from the desk and drew an exact replica of Escher's *Drawing Hands* on the notepad, then I got up, opened the door and slipped out into the corridor. I was on the second floor of what was clearly a busy police station with plenty of cases to solve. The corridor was full of detectives with names like D.S. Cameron and D.I. Caprio hurrying to and fro, all too busy talking on mobiles or checking documents to notice me; in fact, none of them paid me the slightest bit of attention.

Like a midwife after a tricky delivery, I took a deep breath, looked up at the ceiling, relaxed my shoulders and started walking. For some reason, the building felt familiar. Perhaps I'd worked there as a detective some time in the past. Or I might have been a repeat offender, brought in so many times that I knew the place inside out. I might even have been the station superintendent, so well did I know the terrain. Whatever the case, I had no trouble at all in making my way to the stairwell and down the stairs to the basement; and just as I had expected, there was a lockup at the foot of the stairs. It would be jam-packed, I knew, with contraband goods and illegal possessions seized from criminals or suspects brought in for questioning.

The door beckoned me invitingly, so I opened it.

A young officer was sitting behind a counter near the entrance. He seemed to have been crying until just before I went in, but now hurriedly wiped his eyes and looked up at his unexpected visitor.

"Can I help you?" he croaked.

"Ah, this smell brings back memories!" I said as I scanned the back of the lockup. "Thirty years ago, I sat exactly where you're sitting now."

That seemed to reassure the officer, though he still seemed a little uncertain. "Oh, really? So you're actually an old-timer, yes? I always learn a lot from the old-timers."

"OK, OK. That's fine. But tell me. You were crying just before I came in, right? Maybe you're the same as I was. I had my troubles and sorrows, too; actually, I suffered quite a lot. But don't bottle it up – tell me about it. Tell this old-timer why you were crying."

He opened his mouth, but no words would emerge.

"Go on," I insisted. "What could you lose by telling me? That's what old-timers are for, after all. And you're almost like a son to me."

"Well . . . Telling you won't change anything, but . . ." He hesitated for a moment before launching into a full confession. "I've been taking things from the seized property: wristwatches, jewelry, things like that. To pay back loans, you know? I can't afford to live otherwise, not on my pay. But this afternoon there's going to be an inspection by the station superintendent, and he's sure to find out."

"That was a bit stupid of you. Did you sell the things you stole?"

"No. I left them with a pawnbroker."

"Aha. So how much did you get?"

"More than a million yen altogether. Not all in one go."

"Go and buy them back right now." I took the bank envelope out of my pocket and slammed it down on the counter, like the actor Toshiro Mifune might have done. "There's about two million in there. Go now. You can still make it."

The young officer stood up with mouth agape and lower lip quivering. "Th-Th-Thank you!" he eventually cried. "But I don't know if I can ever pay you back. . . ."

"That's OK. Just go. I'll look after things here. If anyone comes, I'll make something up. Go on!"

"All right." He turned back to look at me just as he reached the door. "I can't believe it. It's like something out of a movie."

"This isn't a movie. It's a short story."

The duty officer hurried off, leaving me alone in the seized property lockup. Behind the counter was a central aisle lined on both sides with stacks of shelves. And when I saw what lay on those shelves, I raised my arms and roared hallelujah. For there, arrayed before my giddy eyes, was a veritable hoard of riches: gold, silver and jewels, luxury goods both genuine and counterfeit, arms and ammunition, heroin, cocaine and myriad other substances. In other words, a goldmine of treasures used for all manner of villainy by the most villainous of villains. A catalog of hardware, substances and goods that could only be found here and nowhere else, itching to return to the cozy, corrupt world of capitalist society, liberal society, dark society. Concealing themselves by huddling together in their various volumes and quantities but in reality hoping, wishing, longing, yearning to be discovered and stolen again. And as I was the only person there to steal them, that was just what I did. I first grabbed a Louis Vuitton wheeled carrier case from a shelf full of luxury brand goods, then took a Howa Type 64 automatic rifle from the firearms shelf, dismantled it and put it in the case along with a handful of 7.62 mm caliber NATO bullets from a box magazine. I then selected three P08 semi-automatic pistols

23

and some 9mm-caliber Parabellum cartridges and added them to the mix. That lot alone was enough to make my old arms sag.

I did think of smashing twenty or thirty ornamental vases, but the sheer volume of movables killed my desire to destroy them. So I shuffled out into the corridor, noisily pulling Carrie the carrier case along behind me. Carrie was singing aloud with ecstatic joy to be outside and free at last. With some difficulty I pulled her up the stairs to the first floor and left the station through the front door; no one paid me any attention at all. Though inwardly scolding the police for their sheer criminal negligence, I managed to struggle down the station steps into the street. A taxi was waiting at the roadside. *Go on, get in*, a voice inside me said as I waltzed toward it and climbed in.

I didn't fancy going to Shinjuku this time, as I still had a vaguely nightmarish memory of rampaging through there in the company of phantoms, mental patients, hordes of Chinamen and criminal gangs the previous night. So I asked the driver to take me to Roppongi.

As the taxi moved off, I could wait no longer. With some excitement I pulled the hardware out of Carrie's soft fleshy insides, reassembled the Howa 64, engaged the magazine and loaded the Lugers. Then I took imaginary aim at the crotches of pedestrians on the sidewalk, yelling "Bullseye!" each time.

"Er, sir? What exactly are you doing?" asked the driver, eyeing me in the rear-view mirror.

"Testing the latest weaponry," I replied. "These are just samples. I'll be shifting about ten thousand Howa 64s and thirty thousand Lugers if I'm lucky. Including the ammo they'll fetch around five billion, but in my business that's peanuts. If I manage to sell them all today, I'll treat myself to a solitary toast at *Torikan* in Egota tonight."

"Ah, got you. So when you say Roppongi, you mean the Defence Ministry?"

Er, no. I could imagine the outcome if I were to start brandishing firearms at the Defence Ministry; my rejuvenated body would soon be nothing but an empty honeycomb, the ghastly winds of hell whistling through masses of holes.

"No, not the Defence Ministry," I replied. But then my true destination immediately became clear to me: a place packed to the rafters with people who, though blessed with a modicum of intelligence, use it for nothing but catching cockroaches, who are physically as feeble as koala bears, who have a way with words but only use them to hide their cowardice, who manipulate agricultural quotas, and who are sweet on Chinamen but turn their backs on the film industry, smokers, transgender performers and the elderly.

"Take me to the National Diet Building," I said. The prime minister would be there – the one whose voice annoyed me so. I would shoot him forty-six times. Bullseye.

Bibliography

Suzuki, M., *Gherasim Luca, Strategy of Non-Œdipe* (2009)
Fukuda, T., *Discourse on the Tale of Genji* (1990)
Barthes, R., *The Rustle of Language* (1986)
Ey, H., ed., *L'Inconscient 1* (1966)

Call for the Devil!

"RIGHT. HAVE YOU ARRANGED the tables in a perfect pentangle?" asked the president, voice cracking with emotion.

"I have," replied the marketing director, bottom lip trembling.

"Good. Now place candles on all five points of the pentangle, then light a fire in the middle," said the financial director, face strewn with tears.

"What a cruel, pitiful fate, that we must take such drastic steps to save our company from ruin," the president groaned as he yanked out a handkerchief.

"Yes, but if we don't sell our souls to the devil, 350 workers will be out of a job and fifteen subcontractors will fold," said the marketing director. "In these dark days of financial downturn, there's no other way for a small or medium enterprise to survive!"

"That's right. Did we not vow to hang ourselves?" the financial director sobbed. "We're all going to die, and we're all going straight to hell anyway. So we might as well summon the devil and sell our souls to him first. Then at least we might save all the others we've gotten into this mess with us."

"I agree," agreed the president. "We won't save anyone just by dying. It may be worse than death itself, but we shall sell our souls to the devil first."

"We shall sell our souls to the devil first!" the three all wailed together. "We shall, we shall!"

"So now let us start the ritual for summoning the devil. We'll

27

achieve nothing by standing around crying. Is the fire burning?" asked the president, drying his tears.

"Yes, it is burning good and strong," answered the marketing director.

"So first, please burn this."

"Very well. I shall burn it."

The marketing director took the shriveled body of a lizard from the president's outstretched hand and hurled it into the fire.

"Next, this hen's foot."

"Yes."

"Next, garlic."

"Garlic."

"Next, monkey semen."

"Right."

"Chicken chow mein."

"Chow mein."

"A set square."

"Yes."

"An erotic photograph."

"Yes."

"And finally," said the president, shaking like a leaf as he passed three human hairs to the marketing director. "A hair from each of our heads."

"Y-yes." The marketing director took the three hairs with trembling fingers, closed his eyes, and quickly tossed them into the fire.

There was a bang, and a flash, and a puff of smoke. Then all of a sudden, a human shape started to appear.

"Who hath invoked me, pray?"

Thus spoke the human shape that rose up from the fire, brandishing a halberd as he eyed the three men suspiciously.

"It-It's Benkei!" the president cried in utter stupefaction, doing his best to stop his knees from buckling.

"Sooth, 'tis I. Saito Musashibo Benkei, to be precise, popular figure in Japanese folklore, renowned for my great strength and undying loyalty, my life story both embellished and distorted in kabuki and noh drama – yea, 'tis none other than I!"

The three men all gasped as one.

"And ye three have summoned me? What be then your command?"

"There must be some mistake," called the president. "It was the devil we were after."

"The devil, ye say?" Benkei replied, rolling his eyes madly and stamping his feet in rage. "If there be a devil in these parts, 'tis I who shall rid you of him. Have no fear!"

The three men ducked their heads in terror as Benkei swirled his halberd speculatively through the air.

"I can't see Benkei saving us," the marketing director whispered to the president, their heads still bowed low. "Shall we just ask him to leave?"

"I agree. Let's do that," replied the president. "That's the last thing we want, him ridding us of the devil."

The marketing director threw a cup of water onto the fire, whereupon Benkei vanished without a trace.

"But why did Benkei appear?" asked the bemused financial director.

"Perhaps we got the order wrong," said the president. "Let's change the sequence and try again."

So they cast the ingredients into the fire in a slightly different order. As before, the last to go in were the three hairs from each of their heads. As before, there was a bang, and a flash, and a puff of smoke, and again a human figure rose up from the fire.

"Come to me, all ye who are weary and burdened, and I shall give—"

"Jesus Christ!" the marketing director yelled in bewilderment.

"Ask him to leave," said the president. "God has no place in commerce!"

"Agreed. If we had Jesus on our board, we'd be even deeper in the red," the financial director whined. "He's the friend of the poor, isn't he? He'd only end up siding with the union!"

The marketing director hurriedly dowsed the fire with another cup of water, and Jesus disappeared without a trace.

"God and the devil are kind of related, aren't they? If Jesus

29

can appear, then surely so can the devil," said the president. "Right. Let's try all the different combinations. Sooner or later the devil must appear! Luckily, I prepared a liberal quantity of each ingredient."

So they changed the order again. They changed the amounts. Sometimes they threw whatever came to hand into the fire.

Sometimes nothing happened at all. Sometimes famous characters from past times appeared; sometimes they were fictional, like Joan of Arc, Atom Boy, Beethoven, the Monkey King, and Popeye the Sailor Man. But none of them offered any hope of saving the company from bankruptcy. Some even appeared twice because the men had accidentally burnt the ingredients in the same order – they hadn't been taking notes and had forgotten what combinations they'd already used. In the end, they were just throwing the ingredients together at random. They eventually ran out of monkey semen, then shriveled lizards, then chicken chow mein, in that order. Human figures began to appear less and less frequently in the smoke.

At length, the president came up with a suggestion, inspired partly by fatigue and partly by sheer boredom. "Hold on. We don't all need to be doing this, do we? Why doesn't just one of us carry on while the others get some sleep? Then he can wake the others up if the devil appears."

"You're absolutely right," said the financial director. "Let's take it in turns. I think the marketing director should go first."

So the president and financial director went off to take a nap, leaving the marketing director to continue the ritual alone.

By the time the president and financial director returned the next morning, the fire was nothing but a damp, smoldering mass. The marketing director was sitting with his head in his hands, muttering to himself as if in delirium.

"What happened?" demanded the president. "Why did you let the fire go out? Did no one appear after that?"

The marketing director lifted his face. His eyes were red. "No one appeared at first," he replied dolefully. "I felt so sleepy, but

I continued the ritual. Suddenly, a group of men appeared all at once. I thought they couldn't be the devil as there were too many of them, so I made them disappear. But then . . . Oh no! What have I done?!" He clutched his head in despair. "I regretted it right away, but I couldn't get them back, try as I might. And I was half asleep anyway."

"Well, who were they? This group of men?" asked the financial director.

"They were the Seven Gods of Good Fortune, sailing in a boat laden with gold and treasure. Riches beyond our wildest dreams. We could have paid off all our debts in one go!"

The Onlooker

I STRETCHED MYSELF OUT on the sofa. I was feeling kind of lethargic – not enough exercise, perhaps. But it didn't matter; I've never been that active anyway.

Light from the late afternoon sun came filtering in through the lemon yellow curtains, casting a shadow of lace on the carpet in front of me.

The light was fading. I closed my eyes again. I felt a lot more comfortable than I had done a little while back; my head was starting to clear.

I seemed at last to have understood something that had bothered me for a while – centripetal dependence and centrifugal subordination.

But, of course, this only applies when considering a single, natural center of gravity inside and outside a circle in our perception. What I wanted to consider next was a different problem: whether a specific part of the cosmos could control another part, causing our perceptive activity to be held inside it.

Another thing to bear in mind was that the principle of equilibrium I encountered previously, when considering the problem of dependence within specialization, could also exist in a situation of monarchic subordination. If, for example, we consider the total cosmos as a rectangle constructed under the principle of the golden section and Fibonacci numbers, would a quantitative relationship like 5:8 = 8c 8:(5+8) = 8:13 then become universal?

We will never even begin to elucidate the metaphysical truths of this vast, boundless cosmos until we can solve this enigma.

I was growing tired of my own life view, my view of the world with its microcosmic structure. I needed a new world experience; I needed to keep thinking about these new challenges.

Just at that moment, a woman wearing heavy makeup and a salmon pink dress opened the door to my right and stepped into the apartment from the corridor.

The woman was twenty-seven but looked well over thirty. Fatigue caused by loose living had left conspicuous wrinkles around her eyes. She was physically fit, nonetheless, and exuded sufficient sex appeal to be attractive to men.

She glanced at me then turned back to the corridor. "Come on then!" she called in a slightly husky voice. "What are you dithering out there for?"

Her voice expressed contempt and a degree of arrogance. A man stepped in, hesitantly, nervously, his back bent as if in apology.

The man wore a cheap brown suit and was rubbing his hands together in front of his belly; he seemed to be hiding something. Creases covered his lightly tanned face as he forced a smile in my direction. Whenever I saw this man, past thirty, short, unprepossessing, I felt disgusted. He made me so angry that I got pains in my chest. As always, I ignored him and turned toward the woman. She gave me a little nod before looking back at him.

The look she gave him betrayed a complex of emotions; one was expectation, another anxiety, another still impatience. She expected the man to satisfy her frustrated desires but felt anxious that her prey might escape and so was desperate to make herself as attractive to him as possible.

She held her arms out to him, but he hesitated. His hesitation was so gauche, so pathetic that it was unbearable to watch. The wretchedness of a loser was all too evident in his every move, every shift in his expression. They betrayed the worthlessness of a habitual philanderer who collected adulterous liaisons simply to earn a living.

As he stood there vacillating, he looked over at me again with a faint smile. He almost seemed to be deferring to me; the look in his eyes was one of remorse, as if he were begging my forgiveness.

I felt pity for him. I sighed and lowered my eyes.

The woman glanced at me again then turned back to him. "Take no notice," she said.

He embraced her feebly, then he kissed her. The back of his neck was turned toward me, revealing an ugly scar left by radiation.

Eventually, the woman went to lock the apartment door, then she and the man sloped off into the bedroom, their bodies lasciviously entwined. The door closed and they disappeared from view.

My whole body was sweating; a drop of perspiration rolled down my forehead and along my nose before plopping down onto my lap. I wondered how the same human desires could appear so beautiful in some situations yet so ugly in others. I felt sad when I considered the sheer squalor of human beings, their intentions so plainly visible in their every move. I could understand those intentions quite clearly, and that made me sadder still. For this, I realized, was the very essence of being human; there was no question of forgiving or not forgiving. After all, I would also have to force myself into the same irrational, squalid way of living, one day.

I heard footsteps out in the corridor; someone was trying to open the door. There was a knock.

The woman rushed out of the bedroom in a loose nightgown, carrying the man's clothes in her arms. She was quickly followed by the man, wearing nothing but his underpants.

"It's my husband!" she hissed. "Quick, behind the sofa!"

She pointed to the sofa where I was sitting, so the man ran over and disappeared behind me. The woman hurled the clothes at the man's head then looked at me. "Just stay where you are, there's a love," she whispered, before patting down her tousled hair, walking toward the door and opening it.

A plump man in his forties strode into the apartment wearing a nicely tailored double-breasted suit. He kissed the woman then looked at me and smiled. "Hey there. You OK?" he said in a low, resonant voice. I gave no reply but smiled back stiffly.

He walked straight toward me. I felt a bit uneasy; this man must have some hidden brutality, I thought. On the surface he was mild-mannered, but I knew just by the glint in his eye that he had some hidden brutality. I closed my eyes instinctively.

The woman walked up to him. "I was just taking a nap," she lied, speaking in a shrill voice as if to proclaim her innocence.

The man threw his leather briefcase down onto the sofa next to me.

"I couldn't wait, see. You've never been away this long before," she said, then went to hug him from behind. The man smiled wearily. He took his jacket off and draped it over the briefcase, then turned and embraced her vigorously – unlike the other man. And he kissed her. When they'd finished kissing, the woman flashed a look at the bedroom as if to distract him, then turned back to him. He looked her in the eye. They exchanged glances that burned with naked carnal lust. They nodded to each other, then disappeared into the bedroom together.

The other man, now fully clothed, emerged from behind me. How I pitied him. Once more I could clearly see the radiation scar on the nape of his neck.

He glanced at me; it was as if he wanted to say something. I stared hard at him, but he lowered his eyes. He clearly understood the relationship between us – a relationship that must remain unspoken.

He hurried out into the corridor, making sure his footsteps made no sound. His rounded shoulders reminded me of some timid creature, the terrified quarry of a predator. I felt a terrible sadness for a third time, toward no one in particular.

I looked at the second man's jacket, so casually flung onto the sofa beside me. A letter written in a woman's hand was peeping out of the inside pocket. There was no doubt in my mind; it was from that young woman he'd brought here once, when the other woman was away.

I no longer felt any emotion toward this sordid drama of love and lust acted out by the people around me. Why were they so keen to make their environment even worse than it was already? Why did they seem to enjoy danger so much? It must have been because they needed to assert themselves as living beings, to confirm their very existence. Their emotional torment was like an act of self-abuse; inwardly they were enjoying their suffering, in a masochistic way.

Their personalities had been warped and distorted from the beginning; they were incapable of maintaining them in anything approaching a normal environment. All they were doing was deliberately creating a warped environment, thereby protecting their own warped personalities from derangement.

And this drama was being played out in ordinary homes everywhere, by people who were desperate to make it the social norm.

The woman eventually came out of the bedroom, walked up to me, gently put her hands on my shoulders and kissed me on the lips. I couldn't resist that kiss, with its peculiar watery aftertaste. The kiss of a mother.

"Now, little one. Time for your feed!"

And she thrust the teat of a bottle into my mouth.

It's My Baby

JUST AFTER LUNCH, MY office pal Masada came up to me with a somber look on his face.

"I'm going to have a baby," he said.

"Congratulations!" I replied without thinking. "But hold on. You're not married, are you?"

Masada shook his head dolefully. His massive beer belly swayed perilously close to my nose.

"Actually, it's a bit of a problem," he said. Beads of sweat were breaking out on his chubby red face. "To be honest, I could do with your advice."

I needed a break from the endless tedium of deskwork, so I was only too happy to oblige. "Come on," I said as I grabbed my jacket. "Let's go downstairs."

We sat talking in a coffee shop on the first floor. Business was slow, and we had the place to ourselves.

"So who's the mother?" I asked right away. "Does she want to keep it? Or are you going to break up? You can confide in me, you know."

"Uh, thanks," he replied glumly. "But it's not that kind of problem."

"All right, do *you* want to keep it then?"

"Of course. It's my baby."

"So what's the problem? You both want the baby, so why not just get married?"

"You still don't get it," he said with a sense of rising irritation

39

as he clenched and unclenched his fists on the tabletop. "I'm having the baby. It's me who's pregnant."

I spat out the water I was drinking. "Wh-what? That's not possible!"

"That's what I thought," he said with a mournful shake of his head.

The waitress came to take our order.

"What'll it be?" I asked Masada. "Coffee as usual?"

"No, that would be bad for the baby," he replied in a stage whisper. "I'll have a lemon squash. I have a craving for something sour."

I decided to humor him. "Are you actually going to have this baby, then?" I asked once the waitress had left.

"Of course," Masada replied firmly. "I'm no good at relationships, but I've always wanted kids."

"Not me. I find babies ugly. Grotesque. Just looking at them makes me want to puke. And, anyway, a man having a baby is just wrong. You won't be able to work. It'll drive you mad!"

"I'll be all right. I have the build for carrying a child. I'm 36, so I'm definitely ready for it."

"Right," I said, a little too brusquely. I was getting quite annoyed with the charade. "You asked for my advice, so here it is. Go to the maternity clinic."

"Fine! I'll do that right now," he said as he got up to leave.

We parted outside the coffee shop like grouchy lovers after a tiff.

I went back to my desk but couldn't get it out of my mind. He was joking, right? Or suffering under some delusion perhaps. Men don't have babies, after all – women have a bit of a monopoly on it. Or do they? Could a man actually have a baby? Would it be physically possible? I did some research and discovered that men have actually been known to give birth in the past. But they were all hermaphrodites; they had both male and female organs. Well, I'd seen Masada in the shower at golf, and he definitely had the male ones. But even so, there might still have been room for all the female stuff inside that massive belly of his. And, maybe,

40

one day while he was jerking off, some of his sperm might have hopped back in and fertilized an egg. Just maybe.

But no. It had to be a phantom pregnancy, brought on by his wish to have children. I could imagine all the trouble it would cause if he were really pregnant and he went through with it; how would the baby get out, for starters? Surely not through his rear end, like taking a crap? No, it would have to be delivered by Caesarean section, which would be risky. Masada was good at his job and an asset to the company; we couldn't have carried on without him. I decided to take his claim seriously, and reported it to the department manager right away.

The department manager was more or less frothing at the mouth when he heard about it. He immediately rushed off to inform the general manager. The general manager went into a frenzy and called the president. In the end, it took less than two hours for news of Masada's "pregnancy" to circulate to every department of the company.

Masada returned from the maternity clinic later that afternoon. Ignoring the sideways glances, whispered voices and fingers pointed in his direction, he came straight to my desk with a broad smile on his face; our lovers' tiff was clearly a distant memory already.

"I'm two months pregnant," he reported proudly. He didn't seem to mind the giggles of the office girls in my section. In fact, he went up to one of them and handed her some money.

"Could you get me the latest issue of *Woman's Week*?" he said. "It's got a special feature on baby care."

The girl turned bright crimson, as if she might explode in her attempt not to laugh, then took the money and hurried out into the corridor. No sooner was she out of the door than she burst into uncontrollable laughter.

Masada stopped smoking and drinking – mainly to protect the baby, he said, but also because he started having morning sickness from the third month. Besides alcohol and tobacco smoke, anything with a strong smell would make him feel sick; he would start to gag whenever a colleague reeking of cheap aftershave came anywhere near him. Morning sickness made him irritable, and he was quick to find fault with the office girls.

"Don't come near me wearing that cheap perfume. It makes my stomach turn," he'd say, or "Hey! Go eat your noodles somewhere else!" or "Eurgh! Has your period started? Get away from me!" or "Heck! Your armpits stink! Go away, go home, go anywhere but here!"

How to deal with his pregnancy became quite an issue in the boardroom.

"He's single, isn't he? So the child will be illegitimate. Should we stress the moral angle and have him abort it?"

"No! That would infringe on his rights. He wants to have the baby."

"You say 'the baby', but whose baby is it?"

"His, of course."

"Yes, but it takes two to make a baby."

"I know that."

"So who's the father?"

"You mean, who impregnated him? Good question! Well, I suppose . . ."

"Hey! Don't look at me! Yes, I look after him as my subordinate, but that's as far as it goes!"

"Hmm, you look after him as your subordinate. . . ."

"Come on, don't start that. I'm not gay! Well, I go to gay bars sometimes, but only when I'm drunk."

"How exactly could Masada be pregnant? Has he got a womb or something?"

"Maybe it's in his appendix."

"Or in his ileum."

"Or up his rectum, if he's gay."

"Hey! That's enough of that. The question is: What are we going to do about it? The people in his section say it's interfering with their work. He's so obsessed with the baby that he keeps baring his teeth and snarling at them."

"Like a dog?"

"We'll have to put him on maternity leave and find a replacement quick."

"So no special measures for now?"

"There's nothing else we can do."

Soon, the normally industrious Masada was starting to pay less attention to his work and spending more time looking after his coworkers. A maternal instinct seemed to have awakened inside him; he would brush hairs off the shoulders of male colleagues' jackets, prepare tea for his subordinates, and turn up early to tidy the office. His superiors were aghast, his colleagues were avoiding him, and his subordinates were distracted from their work. The section was grinding to a halt.

We sat drinking coffee downstairs.

"You need to pull your finger out," I advised. "They say you're not doing your job."

"Is that so?" He didn't seem too bothered; in fact, he sounded quite cheerful. "Having a baby changes the way you see things. You would be the same, too."

"Don't be silly. I'm not going to have a baby. But what do you mean? What's different?"

"Going to work suddenly seems pointless. I've only realized since I got pregnant, but the work we do every day is completely meaningless. We were doing the same thing a year ago, and the year before that. But having a baby is the most wonderful thing in the world. In fact, I wouldn't blame women if they just wanted to have babies and nothing else. When they have a baby, nothing else matters, and that's only natural. Compared to that, working in an office is a piece of piss. Remember when we went to that bar and were bragging to the girls there about our company and how important our work is? Well, I'm ashamed of that now. Women cling to the illusion that men's work is more important than theirs, but they don't seem to realize that what *they* do is much more so. I know, because I'm doing both. Having a baby is no joke, I can tell you. No joke at all."

He had a glazed, far-off look in his eyes as he spoke, so I thought it best not to interrupt him. I did think of asking him what exactly was so difficult about having a baby, but I held my tongue as I probably wouldn't have understood anyway.

Some months passed.

One day, Masada came rushing to my desk just as I got back from seeing a client. His face was moist with tears of joy.

"It moved! It moved! The baby! It moved!" he yelled in barely controlled excitement.

Ignoring the scandalized looks of my colleagues, he took off his jacket and loosened his belt.

"Go on, give it a feel!"

"Eurghh! No way!" I said with a grimace. "I might throw up."

"No, you won't! Come on, feel it!" He was almost slobbering with happiness as he undid the top button of his trousers. "Feel it!"

He opened his trousers to reveal a fetching pair of red and white striped long johns underneath. "Come, I don't mind. Feel!"

My hand was trembling as I placed it on his lower abdomen. It felt warm, but nothing was moving.

"It's not moving."

"Of course it is! Put your hand here!" He grabbed my hand and tried to shove it under his long johns.

"Hey, get off me!"

"Please! Put it in!"

"Sorry, but I'm beginning to feel sick."

"You wouldn't if you felt the baby moving," he pleaded. "Please feel it! I'm begging you!"

Still inwardly protesting, I passed my hand down his long johns through a gap he had opened just under his belly button. My fingertips brushed against his coarse pubic hair.

"Well?"

"Your belly button sure sticks out."

"Never mind that. Did you feel it move?"

"No."

"Press harder."

I pressed harder.

"Well?"

Something convulsed under the thick blubber of Masada's lower abdomen. I inadvertently shrieked and leapt back.

"You see? It moved, right?"

With the air of a triumphant matador, Masada turned and started parading his naked belly before the others in the office, laughing inanely as he invited them to have a feel; they all got up from their desks and fled. Thus deprived of willing feelers, Masada turned his attention to the president's office. I jumped up to stop him.

"Don't go in there, he's got a weak heart!" I yelled.

A few more months passed. Masada had been going on about how the baby was getting bigger, but, frankly, it was still hard to see past his old beer belly.

One day, just as the bosses were mulling over how much leave to give him, Masada went into labor – a month too early. The whole office entered panic mode.

"Call the midwife!" "Bring hot water!" "Take him to the sick room!" "Blankets, blankets!"

"It's too late for all that! He'll have to have a Caesarean! Get him to a hospital quick!"

"What happened?" I asked one of the girls in his department.

"He saw a mouse under his desk and his contractions started," she replied. "I didn't think he was the type to be scared of mice!"

Masada was crouching under his desk, gripping his belly and groaning.

"Call a taxi!" I yelled. "Someone go with him! Who has nothing better to do?"

I was the only person with nothing better to do, so I had no option but to help him to his feet and into the taxi.

"Aoyama Maternity Clinic!" I barked at the driver as I eased Masada through the open door. "Please hurry! The baby's almost due!"

"Right!" Startled by our unseemly haste, the driver set off immediately.

"Wife having a baby, then?" he asked a few moments later.

"No. He is," I replied, indicating Masada. "He's having a baby!"

The driver narrowed his eyes and eyed us silently in the rear-view mirror.

"Well?" I asked. "Aren't you surprised?"

The driver said nothing.

"Say something then! Go on, say it! Men don't have babies, right? But you're wrong. Men do have babies sometimes. If women can, why can't men? And a baby with a male mother would have so many talents – maybe more than one with a female mother!"

The driver's eyes were fixed on the road ahead. He had obviously heard enough.

"You think I'm having you on? Like it's some kind of practical joke? Well, it isn't! Do you really think two grown men would invent such an unlikely tale?"

The driver still said nothing.

"For pity's sake, say something! And hey! Don't go taking us to a psychiatric clinic instead, or we'll be late for the operation! He's a man, so he can't give birth normally! Don't you see? Will you please answer me! He's going to have a Caesarean! It's urgent. OK? Driver! Hey, pal! Come on, say something!"

The driver said nothing.

Masada continued to moan and groan, though his labor pains seemed to have subsided somewhat. "We'll make it in time for the surgery, won't we?" he asked, looking at me blearily through half-open eyes.

What could I say? "Of course," I replied.

"I hope it's a boy," he declared. "No. It has to be a boy. I'm sure it is! Oooh! Ouch! Oof!"

As another contraction started, he bellowed like an ox and his usually swarthy complexion turned ruddy brown.

"Urgh! Agggh! Ghh! Oof! Heyurrrgh! Blehhh! Oaargh!"

I tried to comfort him as best I could.

"What makes you think it's a boy?" I asked.

He suddenly seemed to forget his labor pains, sat up in his seat and leaned toward me with a twinkle in his eye.

"I don't know. It's just a gut feeling," he declared with a flourish of his hand.

46

Zarathustra on Mars
A Story for All and None

1. THUS BEGAN ZARATHUSTRA'S DOWNFALL

ONCE, BACK ON PLANET Earth, there was something called a "Nietzsche boom"; people couldn't get enough of the man and his theories about some humans being inherently superior to others. But in the Martian colonies it was more like a "Zarathustra boom". And there was a very good reason for that: no one had ever heard of Nietzsche, that great philosopher from the second phase of earth civilization, but nearly everyone knew of his most famous conception – the philosophical novel *Thus Spake Zarathustra*. By that time, you see, Nietzsche's name had already been washed away by the tides of history and buried under the sands of fashion, along with all his other works. In short, he had become a nobody known by no one. He wasn't mentioned in any literary or philosophical textbook; he had vanished into the distant recesses of the past, far beyond the waves of time that ceaselessly ebb and flow.

But on Mars, in the year 2250, *Zarathustra* came back to life.

For it was in the spring of that year that Kan Tomizuka, Professor of Classical Philography at the Common Knowledge University of Mars, was poring over a pile of ancient books transported from Planet Earth by space container, when he discovered a fragment of *Zarathustra*. The fragment was not written in the original idiom of Nietzsche – that pompous, antiquated style modeled on the classical German of Martin Luther. It had been translated into 21st century Earthspeak, a casual, colloquial mode of speech that had become the global standard by that time.

The professor spent a whole night with the remains of the ancient philosopher's thought, for that was how he liked to do things. Then he started to imagine. If he could translate the fragment into contemporary Marsspeak, he thought, it would definitely be popular and might even become a bestseller.

"I reckon this book will sell like hot cakes," the professor muttered to himself. He'd mistaken the fragment for an autobiography of someone called Zarathustra – an easy mistake to make, in this case, since the cover bearing the original author's name had been ripped off and replaced with a 3-D pinup photo of a 21st-century earth celebrity. In fact, there was nothing to show that it had ever been written by anyone but Zarathustra in the first place.

"I reckon I'll translate this and make it a textbook for the university quadrimester we're in. Then I'll make lots of microreaders and sell them to all the students. Yeah. I'm gonna make a real packet out of this." The professor smiled in self-satisfaction. "Students these days are all so egotistical, so full of themselves. This will be the perfect book for them. I reckon it'll definitely catch on. Yeah, for sure. The young twits will be jumping up to buy it. All I have to do is rewrite it in plain language and make it easy for them to read – obviously, they'd have trouble with the original Earthspeak. That's even a bit hard for me. And I'm a professor! I mean, look at these words he uses: 'vainly glorious' and 'lusty of power'. Yeah, right! Well, I reckon I know what he means. And, anyway, these youngsters are so dim I could make it up and they'd be none the wiser. Yeah. Zarathustra will be a new hero for them. They're gonna love him."

There was no religion on Mars; there were no heroes. Instead, there was a gaggle of B-list celebs, empty-headed idiots who perpetually courted fame and were constantly hounded by the media. In so many ways, young people born on Mars thirsted for a strong, influential leader, one who would show them the way. The way to what? They didn't even know. The professor imagined how gladly the students in the Martian colonies would swallow the book's *Übermensch* ethos of "thoroughly trampling down the ignorant masses." After all, they saw themselves as a kind of élite, having overcome odds of five thousand to one just to get into university. From their lofty heights, the book's popularity would filter down to other young people, people of vernacular learning, and even people with ordinary common sense. Eventually, it would spark a Zarathustra boom, and everyone would be falling over themselves to buy it. At least, that's what the professor thought.

So he started translating the book. Of course, it was impossible for the professor to extract the profound and weighty meaning of Nietzsche's original from the dumbed-down phrasing used in the 21st-century Earthspeak version. So he just converted it to modern speech as best he could, made it even easier to understand, amended and corrected it, inserted the odd colloquialism, and peppered the text with jokes. For nothing would work without jokes, after all.

To make Zarathustra even more accessible to the ordinary reader, he decided to rewrite it as a first-person novel. He excised various problematic parts, like the book's attack on religions and their obsession with the afterlife, and its treatise on the irrational emotionality of women. He judged the former to be irrelevant on Mars, where there was no religion, and the latter to serve no purpose but to annoy his female readers.

In a state of considerable excitement, the professor translated Part I of *Zarathustra* straight through in the span of only three days from February 30th to 33rd, 2250.

This is how his translation went.

Zarathustra's Story
by Zarathustra (translated by Kan Tomizuka)

Hi, guys!

Name's Zarathustra, that's *Zara-too-stra*, but you can call me Zaz.

I'm gonna tell you a real cool story now.

When I was thirty, I left the place where I was living. I worked for a soft drink outfit, but they gave me the boot. So I went into the mountains and started living there. I did as I pleased and wandered about for a bit. Ten years, actually.

What's that? I must've got bored? No way. But after ten years, I did have a bit of a change of heart. One morning, I woke up early, which was unusual for me, and went outside. Just then, the sun was coming up over the horizon, and I was like, *Wow*! You know? See, on Planet Earth the sun rises in the east and looks all red. Not like it does on Mars, or somewhere.

So anyway, I looked up at the sun and said:

"Respect, sun, you rule! Yeah, you rule in the heavens up there. Looks like you're having a real cool time too. But you know what? I bet you wouldn't be so glad if you didn't have no one to shine on! Eh? For the last ten years, I've seen you shining on this simple fiberglass dome what I live in. But if it wasn't for me, my mutant canary and my artificial baby terrapin, you would've felt a bit stupid going up there in the sky every day and going down in the evening, sometimes getting partly hidden behind clouds and that. Yeah, I'm sure you would've. Me and my mutant canary and my artificial baby terrapin, we waited for you every morning, like your trusty pals. We let you shine on us, and I thought, jeez, that guy's real lucky having people like us for friends. But, come to think of it, sun, I'm a bit like you, you know? I'm so clever. I'm a genius like an electronic brain crammed full of data, a bit like a bee that's gathered too much honey on its little hind legs. Yet no one knows anything about me. Well, we can't be having that, can we? There must be a lot of people who would, like, give their right arm to know what I know. So, just like you, I wanna find them, find all them people what envy my wisdom. I'm gonna find them people what think they're

50

clever and show them how stupid they are. I'm gonna teach them, you know, like stupid people should just listen to what other people say, and then they'll be happy. I'll teach it to the poor folks, tell them what I know and make them happy. So I'm gonna go back down there, down to where all the common people live, where they all live on top of each other. . . ."

The professor was not wrong in his surmise. The good citizens of Mars, where dumbing down was already an advanced art form, were delighted with this style of delivery addressed directly to the reader *and* in words they could understand. The book was advertised as "philosophy anyone can dig." As a result, it was not only a hit with students; the ordinary masses and lovers of dumbed-down culture were practically breaking down doors to buy the microreader. They didn't want to miss out on the latest trend, after all. For them, the fact that there was a "philosophy" they could discuss in the workplace and at home was something very cool, very wicked indeed. No one questioned the authenticity of the work; like all elaborate hoaxes, *Zarathustra* played on people's reluctance to show their ignorance, or what could be called "the Emperor's new clothes effect." Some university dons even claimed to have met Zarathustra and to have debated the nature of morality with him.

And it didn't stop there. In his university lectures and general education classes on 3-D TV, the professor dropped hints that this Zarathustra was actually still alive on Earth. Zarathustra's name started to spread amongst intellectuals and even filtered down to the lowbrows through weekly 3-D photo readers. Women began to idolize Zarathustra's unseen image. And as in any other era, there were some who fancied themselves artists or philosophers, and many of them became ardent "Zarathustrophiles". One charitable group even started collecting donations in the hope of inviting Zarathustra to Mars.

Zarathustra stayed at the top of the bestseller list for several months. Special documentaries about the book were shown on

51

3-D TV, microscanners and 3-D microreaders, and Professor Kan Tomizuka was hauled in front of the cameras each and every time. For this, he instantly joined the ranks of celebrity.

Having once mentioned that Zarathustra was a real, living person, the professor was now obliged to specify, in every interview and in considerable detail, exactly where on earth Zarathustra was living and what he was doing there. In the process, an image of Zarathustra gradually started to crystallize in the professor's own mind. Before long, he actually started to believe the bogus Zarathustra he himself had fabricated.

One day, a handling clerk at Mars Spaceport was making a routine check of the passenger list on a scheduled mission from Earth to Mars via Lunar City. He was astonished to find, among the 3-D photos of the passengers, that of a man called Zarat Huistra.

"It's Zarathustra!" he cried.

The face of the man in the photograph, handsomely tanned, a gleam in his eye, chin held high with pride, was definitely the Zarathustra the clerk knew so well. For it was beyond a shadow of doubt the Zarathustra he'd seen in a composite portrait on a microscanner. The clerk hurriedly contacted all television stations by Visifone and showed them the man's photograph.

"Zarathustra's coming on the next scheduled flight!"

"No! Really?"

"Yeah! It's him!"

"Hey, that's just . . . Er . . . Y'know?"

In next to no time, Mars Spaceport was heaving with media people.

And before too long, a tiny silver speck appeared in the night sky over Mars, then gradually grew in size until it was clearly visible as the scheduled passenger-freight mission from Earth. Retro-boosters blazed as the craft descended onto the Spaceport's landing pad. Photographers in spacesuits flocked to the airlock hatch. Around them gathered a throng of Zarathustra fans and students, who came rushing in with *Welcome Zarathustra!* signs.

Some minutes later, the landing pad was enclosed by its

retractable dome and the air inside it filled with oxygen. A few passengers stepped out. And there behind them, now standing on the steps of the hatch, was Zarat Huistra – or Zarathustra, as he would now be called. Everyone in attendance let out a great cheer. Zarathustra wore the overalls of a sub-B-grade Earth laborer and held a battered suitcase in his hand.

At first, he didn't seem to realize that the cheers from the waiting hordes were directed at him. He could see his name written (badly, he thought) on the welcome signs, but for the longest time he just stood there stunned. Even when he was surrounded by journalists and showered with generous words of welcome from so many eager mouths, he still looked as if he just didn't get it. Three days of stubble stood proud on his chin.

One insightful journalist, somewhat disappointed at Zarathustra's appearance, had a thought. *Looks like this man ain't that famous on Earth after all*, he mused. *Maybe that's why he's so surprised at getting a welcome like this. Actually, he don't look that special anyway. But who cares about Earth? This is Mars, and on Mars he's famous. We can't afford to ignore him and let our rivals get the scoop!*

The journalist immediately adjusted the high-performance microphone on his lapel and called out to Zarathustra. "Welcome to Mars!" he started. "Why was you fired from your job?"

Startled by the question, Zarathustra replied with one of his own. "Wazzat? How come you know I was fired?"

"Your story's way popular over here. We know all about you!"

"Kidding, yeah? Jeez. But what's all this melee, bro?"

"Well, of course, it's because everyone wants to see you!"

"Way cool. I sure as hell was not expectin' that."

"So, can you tell us what brings you to Mars today?"

"Yeah, sure. It's that old Earth Shuttle, man." A ripple of laughter coursed through the crowd.

"No, no. I meant, why have you come?"

"Oh. Well, I reckoned there might be some work in these parts, yeah? I got fired, see."

"Yeah, we know about that. So we have a proposal for you.

How would you like to be a lecturer on our social education program?"

"Way to go, bro. What's the bread like?"

"You'll do all right. You can be sure of that."

"OK, cool. What's that you say? Lecherer? No sweat. Can do."

—And thus began Zarathustra's downfall.

2. THUS SPAKE ZARATHUSTRA

PROFESSOR TOMIZUKA WAS INTERVIEWING "Zarathustra" in the lobby of the Hercury Hotel. An astute executive at MBC, the planet's major broadcaster, had arranged the event. All the other media companies had flocked to grab a piece of the action, but MBC was now in the driving seat. A throng of half-crazed fans milled around outside the building, and a line of security guards made sure they couldn't lower the tone of this great meeting of minds.

Professor Tomizuka was the only person on Mars who knew the truth – that the man they were calling "Zarathustra" was in fact a fake. But he had no intention of exposing the man's true identity; on the contrary, he did his best to support and encourage him. He came to his rescue with timely comments here and there, all designed to pull the wool further over the viewers' eyes. This thickset, stubborn, unshaven man could easily have been mistaken for a laborer, but he fitted the professor's image of Zarathustra exactly. If he could make him a media celebrity, the professor's star would surely rise as well.

"Hi!" he started, doing his best to mimic Zarathustra's style of speech. "I'm Kan Tomizuka, the dude what translated your autobiog. I'll show you the book later if you like."

"Don't follow you, bro, but, hey, keep jivin', man!"

"Yeah, right. Anyway, there's loads of young dudes and chicks on Mars that completely dig your philosophy, man."

"Young dudes these days ain't good," said Zarathustra. "They sure is good at talkin', but they can't do nothin' real. I don't dig young dudes. Chicks are OK, though. They're cool."

"Yeah, get you, get you. I know all about you and your liking for chicks. Like, you wrote about it in your book? What was it now? Oh yeah, 'Am I saying you should curb your instincts? The hell I am! Am I saying you should say no to sex? Well, some people say that's cool, but for some it would be like losin' an arm. So here's my advice. If you can't say no to sex, then don't try to. Just say yes'. That last bit's real popular with them young dudes and chicks these days."

"No shit. Couldn't have said it better. What dude wrote that, then?"

"Come on, man! That's all things you said, ain't it?"

"Oh yeah . . . Is it?"

"Jeez, you sure is good at acting dumb."

Everyone in the lobby laughed. Then one of the journalists had a thought. *Yeah, acting dumb*, he reasoned. *I bet that's his game. Shrewd move, dude. Even the way he talks, all slang and street talk. Cool or what? That'll push the ratings up, and he sure knows it.*

Later that night, Kan Tomizuka visited Zarathustra in his luxury suite at the Hercury Hotel. He asked Zarathustra to read the translation of the book he was supposed to have written – and thus started the process of "educating Zarathustra". As it happened, Tomizuka had every reason for haste; the first episode of MBC's *Learn with Zarathustra* was due to be aired just three nights later. In the program, Zarathustra was supposed to explain the book in words everyone could understand. So it wouldn't be a bad idea if he understood the book himself.

It would, of course, be far too tedious to go into detail about the desperate measures the professor took to educate Zarathustra over the next three days; suffice to say that his efforts bore fruit, in a manner of speaking. In fact, the first TV broadcast had an explosive impact on the whole of Mars. The professor's translation shot back to the top of the bestseller list. Zarathustra fans doubled in number, a fan club was formed, and teenagers fought tooth and nail to get their hands on Zarathustra's 3-D portrait.

As the broadcasts continued, Zarathustra grew increasingly adept at explaining his own "philosophy" – and revealed himself to be quite an actor in the process. His stern expression, gravelly voice and sturdy physique gained popularity with the pale, delicate young ladies born of electronic civilization on Mars; his candor and honesty won the trust of the planet's children. His goofy sense of humor was well received by light culturalists, while some students even appreciated what he actually said.

Zarathustra's performance was always accompanied by wildly exaggerated gestures.

"It's a real hot day, right, and I'm sleepin' under a fig tree in this, like, *orchard*. Yeah? And I'm puttin' my arm over my face like this. Then whaddaya know but this adder comes and bites me on the neck, just *there*. You know what an adder is, right? It's a kind of poisonous snake. Yeah. And it bites me, and I'm like *AAARGHH!!!* and screamin' in pain, on account of like it hurts and that. And then I'm looking at this snake, and, you know, like it's an *adder*, right? But that snake takes one look at my mad face and tries to get the hell outta there! Wrigglin' away like a good 'un! So I say to the guy, 'Hey! What kinda adder are you? You oughta be ashamed of yourself. Snakes don't run away, man!' And I'm like sayin' that for real, right? But then I think, well, at least he woke me up in time an' that. I was gonna be late for work! So I say to him, 'Respect, snake! I owe you one.' Then whaddaya think that snake boy does? He gives me this real guilty look and says, 'Jeez, man, I'm real sorry. You're Zaratoostra, aincha? If I'da known it was you, I would never have bitten you. No way, man! Well, I really am sorry, boss, but you won't be doin' no work today, no sirree. 'Cos you see, my venom is lethal. This venom in these here fangs, yeah? It's *LEE – THAL*. You're gonna die, man!' So I say to that snake boy, 'Get outa here, you gotta be kiddin!' And I smile at him. 'You know who I am, dontcha? I'm *Zaratoostra*, that's who I am! Guy as big as me don't get killed by no snake venom, no way Jose. But hold on now. You gone done a real bad thing there. How you gonna 'pologize for *that*?' And then he starts shakin', that snake boy, he starts shakin'. And he says, 'Boss, I'm real sorry I didn't recognize you before. Tell you what I'm gonna do. I'm gonna suck that venom right out of you, so I am, so help me God and hope to die. Amen.' And he comes up to me and starts suckin' the wound on my neck."

Now a student piped up with a question: "And what exactly is the moral of this story?" Of course, the question was also part of the script.

"That's a good question," replied Zarathustra. "What I'm tryin' to say is, when someone takes a swing at you, you gotta take a swing back! If someone done somethin' bad to you, you don't just sit there sayin' nothin', or turn the other cheek, or that kinda thing. Makin' him feel ashamed ain't gonna do no good. What you gotta do is get *MAD*! Those guys that, like, *accept* bein' smacked by other guys like they're some kinda saint, some kinda holy Booda, that typa guy really gets up my nose. If some guy smacks you, you gotta smack the guy back. That's the only way, I'm tellin' ya. 'Cos, y'see, it's more humaner to get your own back than not do nothin' at all."

Thus spake Zarathustra.

3. THUS SANG ZARATHUSTRA

AS ZARATHUSTRA'S POPULARITY GREW, TV stations and microscanner companies on Mars started competing with each other to sign him up. The result was that, despite an unwritten agreement between the companies to keep costs down, his appearance fee rose to outrageous proportions. And that, of course, generated a sizeable income for his manager and mentor, Professor Kan Tomizuka.

Other ingenious ways were devised to cream money from ordinary people. One advertising company thought up a "Zarachat" messaging service. Ingenious! Zarathustra fans would pay a small fee to send a message card to their hero and would get a personally signed reply from him in return. Little did they know that Zarathustra never saw any of the cards; they were processed by a room full of operators trained to mimic Zarathustra's official signature. The fans were happy with their reply card, while the advertising company and card publisher each made life-changing fortunes from the venture.

Zarathustra became a talk show host on MBC, the same channel that had previously aired *Learn with Zarathustra*. No matter who the guest was, Zarathustra always stole the show – he was just too popular. But that didn't matter as it more than doubled the channel's ratings. Zarathustra made no attempt to soften his blunt style of questioning, his acid tongue or his brash attitude; all his guests received the same breezy treatment, whatever their status. The viewers were, of course, delighted to see that.

One night, the Earth Shuttle exploded on liftoff, killing 1,832 passengers and crew. MBC rushed Zarathustra to the scene, where he immediately took over the live coverage, interviewed the victims' relatives in his usual uncompromising style, then gathered them together and started preaching his philosophy to them. Understandably angered, the relatives attacked Zarathustra *en masse*. He ended up spending a week in hospital, but the broadcast hit new heights of popularity with viewers.

Zarathustra also appeared on other channels, mainly as a contestant on game shows. He always took more camera shots than the host and regular contestants, and, of course, commanded a much higher fee.

With his increasingly monumental wealth, Zarathustra built a mansion on prime housing land in a residential dome. He called it Zarathustra Heights, and his eccentric lifestyle there soon became a rich topic of conversation. He got into the habit of proposing marriage on the spot to any beautiful woman he met, starting with the singer Matilda Trumpet. This sparked a succession of romantic scandals and rumors, cannon fodder for the tabloid press.

Then the director of the most popular TV show on Mars invited Zarathustra to sing on his program, more out of courtesy than anything else. Zarathustra's performance was surprisingly well received. Now even the record companies were vying for his signature.

Eventually, the single "Through the Night with Zarathustra" (lyrics by Kan Tomizuka) was released, selling two million copies overnight. Soon it was impossible to go anywhere on Mars without hearing it. In a deep, virile voice Zarathustra sang:

It's the night, yeah!
It's the night,
When all them lovin' dudes sing.
Them stars all a-twinklin', yeah
Them worms all a-glowin', yeah
They all want the light
But I don't want no light, no way
What I want's the night
So listen when I say
I don't wanna be the light
I wanna be the night
Oh yeah
Through the night with Zarathustra!

That made the record company executives sit up. So then the songwriters churned out a string of smash hits for the man, each one a million-selling sensation.

Now a movie company, Total Scope, came up with an idea for a musical based on "Through the Night with Zarathustra". Of course, they had Zarathustra penciled in for the lead role. But Kan Tomizuka wasn't so sure; he didn't think Zarathustra could carry the part, so he turned the proposal down. Undaunted, Total Scope persuaded the professor to sell the music rights and went ahead with the movie anyway, using top Martian actor Bart Krummschnauze in the lead. Zarathustra nevertheless agreed to dub the songs and appeared as a waiter in a couple of scenes. His appearance caused quite a stir; he acted with surprising aplomb, for a waiter. So when Total Scope came up with the idea for the next musical movie, *Zarathustra Memories* with Zarathustra himself as the lead, Kan Tomizuka did not hesitate to accept the idea and a very handsome check.

The film broke all box office records, aided by the popularity of the title song; *Zarathustra Memories* had won a Hammy a few days before the film's release. The film's success ushered in a new dawn for the Martian film business, which until then had been regarded as a sunset industry.

Keen not to lose out on the next big thing, television companies started planning new TV shows for Zarathustra, besides his current affairs programs *Good Morning Zarathustra* and *Zarathustra Chews the News*. As well as *The Zarathustra One-Man Show*, the viewing public could now enjoy his many talents in a serial TV drama.

Zarathustra and his manager Kan Tomizuka consequently found themselves surrounded night and day by promoters, agents, producers, rumors, wads of notes and endless cups of coffee.

Of course, Zarathustra also appeared in commercials, as there were more and more products and services bearing his name. That Zarathustra should appear in person to endorse these products and services was only natural. "It's my kinda thing," he would croon, or "Look like me, be like me!"

After completing five movie musicals, Zarathustra came to Kan Tomizuka with a proposition. He wanted to appear in a film without music – a serious film, a drama, a thriller even. He reckoned he had the talent to pull it off. Word leaked to the executives at Total Scope, who immediately commissioned a serious script for him. What would be the best vehicle for his talent as a serious actor? Why, *The Legend of Zarathustra*, of course. And of course, both Zarathustra and his manager Kan Tomizuka agreed to the proposal wholeheartedly.

In advance of the film's release, a fashionable author was commissioned to write a novel based on the script. Unlike the lofty work originally translated by Kan Tomizuka, this was melodrama, pure and simple. Then, to coincide with the production of the movie, the novel was serialized on a microscanner and released in book form a week before the film's première. The novel sold five million copies, and the film won the Golden Ribbon at the Mars Film Festival. But because the story was slightly more serious this time, box office takings were down compared to the previous five films.

"I reckon we should've stuck to the other type," the professor said to Zarathustra.

Zarathustra agreed; he had already racked up crippling debts with his playboy lifestyle and was far more interested in making money than winning prizes.

So now, more Zarathustra movies were made in the "light entertainment" style. These proved so popular that more and more money was poured into each one. Sets became increasingly extravagant, and soon Zarathustra was starring in historical epics and big-budget productions. The cost of producing these blockbusters grew to such astronomical proportions, in fact, that executives at Total Scope started to think twice about making films with Zarathustra in the lead role.

So now the 3-D television companies started commissioning low-budget sci-fi series from independent production companies. Zarathustra played the lead as usual, but he was now a cartoon character fighting comic-strip adversaries: King Kong, Godzilla, and the Pod People from Pluto, among others. If anything, these TV series found greater popularity with the Martian masses than the films had done; children loved them. The result was, of course, that feature film versions were soon made, and Zarathustra once again appeared in Martian cinemas.

That was when people started to get tired of him. There was, after all, only so much they could take.

4. THUS WENT ZARATHUSTRA BACK TO THE MOUNTAIN

ZARATHUSTRA EARNED A LOT of money. He also spent a lot of money – the scores of beautiful women who constantly surrounded him made absolutely sure of that. His thirst for riches and the trappings of riches led him into the clutches of criminal organizations and high-interest loans, which left him increasingly out of pocket.

Zarathustra wasn't completely stupid. He could see that his

star was fading and his popularity waning. So, in a bid to prop up his ratings, he hurriedly engineered a marriage to the famous actress Marsha Goldmine. The wedding was suitably extravagant and hyped by all the major 3-D TV companies, but the sad fact was that Zarathustra had dug himself an even deeper pit of high-interest debt just to pay for it. To make matters worse, the marriage was broken off after only one week due to Zarathustra's infidelity. The exorbitant alimony demand was the start of his real downfall.

Zarathustra's life thereafter spiraled ever downward into an abyss of depravity. He would get drunk in bars and start fights with other customers, smash chairs over their heads and cause grievous bodily harm. Many was the night he spent in custody.

But it was the incident with the ray gun that finally sealed his fate. Possession of ray guns was forbidden on Mars, but when it emerged that Zarathustra had bought one from an Earth smuggler, he was arrested. In the end, he got off with a fine, but the incident destroyed his standing as a celebrity. Loose living was one thing, but the gentle inhabitants of Mars simply could not abide public figures tainted with the smear of ray gun ownership. Zarathustra was finished.

TV companies started the process by ending his regular appearances on their programs. Commercials for products bearing his name were pulled, and the products themselves were binned as no one wanted them any more. Kan Tomizuka was quick to dissociate himself from his erstwhile charge; and as no university wanted the professor's services any longer, he contented himself with setting up a small talent agency and started touting fresh prospects.

Zarathustra sold off his luxury air car, his house-cleaning robot, and his house, thereafter spending every night in seedy watering holes where he drowned himself in Martian liquor.

He still received requests for public appearances – but only from transgender strip joints in an E-grade residential dome, where he occasionally took the stage as Madame Zarathustra or appeared in the nude show "Zarathustra Decameron". Even then, his constant drinking backstage invariably caused problems. The end finally came when he flew into a rage at the abysmal appearance fee, beat up a female artiste and tried to strangle a stagehand. The promoter reluctantly called in the mob and had him thrown out of the dressing room door into the back street, where he lay pitifully crumpled in a pool of his own vomit mixed with artificial Martian rain.

For several months after that, residents of the E-grade residential dome reported seeing a tramp, much the worse for drink, sprawled across sidewalks in the back streets. On being woken from his drunken torpor, he would yell, "Y'know who I am? I'm Zarathustra, that's who I am!"

The Martian mass media were quick to create new celebrities, but, if anything, they were even quicker to forget them; less than a year after Zarathustra had been removed from public view, hardly anyone could even remember his name.

Three years passed.

Zarathustra had disappeared from the E-grade residential dome; there was not a single person who knew where he was or what he was doing.

The last time 3-D television viewers ever saw Zarathustra was on an MBC program called *Where on Mars Are They Now?* Near the end of the broadcast, his image appeared for just four seconds on the 3-D screen. He was shoveling garbage on a landfill mountain in the waste-processing dome. And as he brandished his shovel, he sang. What did he sing? He sang *The Zarathustra Rap*:

Yo, Zarathustra, go, Zarathustra, go, Zarathustra, bro'
Yo, Zarathustra, go, Zarathustra, go, Zarathustra, go!

Having a Laugh

"I SEE THOSE SUNSPOTS have increased again. Have you heard from the Smithsonian?"

"No, they must be scratching their heads as well. There was supposed to be a solar wind at the solar maximum four years ago, but it never happened. I'd never known such a weak solar cycle, and other scientists must have felt the same. They were all saying it was the start of a diminished cycle that could last for decades."

"So the sunspots are a kind of reaction to that? It's like the sun has caught smallpox."

"Don't be unscientific. Sunspots do not occur as a kind of reaction to anything. Now then, have we had any news from that satellite that's observing the sun's magnetic field? You know, High Node-chan?"

"It's Hinode-chan."

"Huh. Silly names made up by anime nerds. The guys at NASA are involved in that project too, aren't they? Have we had any contact from them?"

"I don't know. But if you ask me, it looks like a huge magnetic field has been generated by differential rotation."

"There's a massive magnetic force out there, that's for sure. Most of those spots are larger in diameter than this whole planet – it's terrifying. They could generate a solar wind with catastrophically destructive force."

"Shouldn't we tell the government?"

"I think we should."

"Prime Minister, airports around the world are in crisis because satellites are shorting out. Planes are straying from their flight paths and going all over the place."

"That sounds serious. Can't they just land somewhere?"

"When they try to land, they can't lower their landing gear, or they deviate from the runway because their electronic systems have gone wrong. There have been some terrible accidents."

"Why has all this happened? What are the experts and scientists saying?"

"Something about a solar wind being generated and charged particles being discharged toward the earth."

"I've been trying to use my mobile for ages but can't get a signal. Is that related?"

"Yes. They say the charged particles are jamming cell phone signals. The whole world is in turmoil. Cars that rely on satellite navigation are going crazy and crashing into each other."

"It's a state of emergency. M-martial law. Invoke martial law. And a curfew. No one allowed in the streets after sundown!"

"Something's heading this way from south-southeast. Looks like Sea Shepherd."

"What on earth for? They should know this is just a survey. Certainly not 'whaling for scientific purposes'. After all, that's been banned by the International Court of Justice in The Hague. Don't they know this isn't scientific whaling?"

"They may be tracking us just to make sure. Oh, look! A gigantic shoal of fish to the southwest. Hey, there are masses of them! Wait a minute, they're wh-wh-whales! A massive pod of whales! We can't survey anything in this state. Maybe the Sea Shepherd ship is trying to protect them."

"This is abnormal. Call the captain. If we stay on our present course we'll collide with the whales, unless Sea Shepherd collides with them first."

"What is it?"

"Captain, take a look. Masses of whales, heading this way!"

"Ah! Minke whales, I'd say. And some Bryde's. Baleens too. My, oh my. Hold on, that's odd, isn't it? Why are different species of whale swimming together, like it's some kind of rush hour?"

"Captain, they're not swimming. They're charging northeast, as if something's driving them away."

"Well, whatever. Let's just make sure we avoid them. Hard to port!"

"Hard to port!"

"Hard to port!"

"Oh, look, there are even some sperm whales. Fin whales too. My, oh my."

"And over there – blue whales! They're on the verge of extinction, aren't they?"

"This is abnormal. Abnormal I say. Something must have messed with their sense of direction."

"Do you think that huge magnetic field all over the planet could have anything to do with it?"

"It must do. That would also explain why our communications have broken down and we can't contact anyone."

"Oh no! The Sea Shepherd ship has collided with the whales! It's a complete wreck! No one could possibly have survived that!"

"Let's pray for their souls."

"Captain, wake up. Wake up!"

"Judy? Ah, Judy. What is it? What's the matter?"

"We can't get a signal from the GPS satellites. Autopilot has gone south, and the sensors and gyrocompass aren't working properly."

"What's our location right now?"

"All I know is we're over the sea. I caught a glimpse through the clouds just now."

"What could that mean? If it's the Indian Ocean then we're still on course. How about communications?"

"Gone. That's the problem. We can't communicate with anyone."

"Why didn't you wake me earlier?"

"Sorry. You seemed to be having such a good time there with Judy."

"The only thing we can do is change to manual and reduce altitude. We need to confirm our location."

"If the passengers start kicking up, we won't be able to respond unless we're on autopilot."

"And how can we respond if they do start kicking up? It would be futile. There are 280 lives at stake here, and our duty is to save them."

"Captain! We're losing altitude, but we're not on manual! The plane's out of control! Even if we find an airport, we won't be able to circle or start an approach, let alone land!"

"I know that!"

"Oh, dear. The sea. I can see the sea! We're going to fall into the sea and die. My body will be found at the bottom of the sea, right next to the black box."

"Didn't you learn how to deal with near-death situations at college? Calm down."

"I'm going to sing."

"You don't have to sing."

"Captain! Unless it's a mirage or some kind of hallucination, I see land ahead!"

"Ah. I recognize the topography. I've flown here many times in the past – it's the Gulf of Oman. What you see ahead is the United Arab Emirates."

"Maybe we could somehow land at Dubai Airport? I long to piss in the golden urinals they have there."

"By all means do. Aah. If only we had a flight engineer, like in the good old days."

"Hey! There's Dubai! I can see Dubai!"

"But we're not heading for the airport – we should be going a bit more north-northwest for that."

"We're already flying too low. We're going to hit the city, aren't we?"

"Don't cry. Let's just try to avoid a major catastrophe. Aah. If only we had a self-destruct button."

"Self-destruct? Not on my watch!"

"But we're going to die anyway!"

"Yes, of course. Human destiny is to die, but our instinct is to stay alive as long as we possibly can, even if only for one second."

"Quit the pointless philosophy."

"Hey, Captain! What's that over there? That tall building up ahead?"

"It's the Burj Khalifa, the highest structure in the world."

"We're heading straight for it. It'll be a disaster. It'll start a world war, Captain! People will say it's revenge for 9/11! Revenge on Islam from the capitalist West! And to make matters worse, this is an American Airlines plane, the same as the one that hit the North Tower of the World Trade Center!"

"Do we have a self-destruct mechanism?"

"Captain, let's sing. Let's sing a song we both know, together."

"Do you know 'You're Driving Me Crazy?'"

"Yes. My grandpa used to sing it."

"So, let's sing."

"*You're Driving Me Crazy. What did I do? What did I do?*"

* * *

That evening, I dined at an Italian restaurant with friends. We had quite a lot to drink. By the time the pasta arrived, we were already churning out corny puns like "Al dente cantabile!"

I left the restaurant at around midnight and arrived home about an hour later. As I had an early start the next morning, I would normally have got breakfast ready before turning in. But I was too far gone to do that, and just collapsed on the bed.

For some reason, I couldn't get to sleep. So I thought of this story.

Daniel was a prince. One night when he was fifteen, his uncle Timothy, the duke, came into his bedroom and said, "The king is dead, so tonight there will be an all-night council to decide his successor. Of course, it could be you. Depending on the result tomorrow morning, I will give you this Cartier watch." The duke grinned as he showed Daniel a golden watch.

It was indeed a splendid watch. When Daniel saw it, he wanted it really badly. But why did the duke mention the watch before the successor had been decided? Daniel was puzzled.

The duke left the room.

The next morning, the duke came into Daniel's bedroom with a big smile on his face. "Good morning, Daniel," he said. "Regrettably, the decision went to your older half-brother Arthur. So, as promised, here is the watch." And he handed Daniel the watch he'd shown him the night before.

Daniel was surprised. "But, Uncle, I'm not the successor. Why are you giving me the watch?" he asked.

The duke gave a knowing smile. "If you had been chosen, you wouldn't have been given the watch," he replied in a low whisper.

Though not fully comprehending their meaning, Daniel never forgot the shock of hearing those strangely ominous words. When he was sixteen, he still remembered them. When he was seventeen, he still remembered them. And now he was twenty.

One night, his uncle Timothy, the duke, came into his bedroom and said, "King Arthur is dead, so tonight there will be an all-night council to decide his successor. Of course, it could be you. Depending on the result tomorrow morning, I will give you this Piaget watch." The duke grinned as he showed Daniel a golden watch.

This too was a splendid watch, more splendid even than the Cartier watch. When Daniel saw it, he wanted it really badly. But this time he was likely to be chosen as the successor, and if that happened, he might not be given the watch. On the other hand, if he became king, he could make decisions about everything – including the watch.

Daniel said nothing. The duke gave a knowing smile as he left the room. Daniel tried to sleep but couldn't; he kept thinking about the watch and that weirdly ominous smile. What was to become of him?

The next morning, I got up, went into the kitchen and made breakfast.

* * *

That day, my boss had been bawling me out because we'd screwed up a delivery to an important client. It hadn't even been my fault, but I was ordered to go to Gunma early the next morning to patch things up with the client. As a result, my whole body was tingling with destructive impulses by the time I left the office. I stopped at a local pub to eat dinner and drown my sorrows before making my way home.

As soon as I opened the front door, the intruder alarm started beeping. It always did that, but the noise was unusually irritating this time. I inserted the key to switch it off. Then I heard an audio message, cheerfully announced in a young woman's voice:

"Please check the flashing display."

I'd forgotten to close the door behind me. With mounting frustration, I slammed the door shut before putting the key back in.

"Welcome home."

When things were going well, I found the voice reassuring. But now it was just annoying. I tend to make idiotic blunders when I'm agitated, so I decided to calm myself by soaking in a hot bath. First, I went to the bedroom to set the hot water temperature. I pressed the button a few times until the display reached 41 degrees. From the bathroom, I could hear the woman's voice telling me what I'd just done.

"The water temperature has been raised."

Yes, I know that. Next, I pressed the 'Bath auto' button.

"Your bath is now filling."

All right, all right! Why do you have to keep talking in that posh accent? Couldn't you say something in local dialect for a change? My frustration was really spilling out now. The voice guidance system had been installed all over the house – not only in the intruder alarm and hot water system but also in the telephone, cooker and various other household appliances. And for some reason, they all used the same woman's voice.

"Your bath will be ready in three minutes."

Who the hell are you anyway? Have you cornered the market in voice recordings or something? OK, so how about talking in a cute voice for once?

"Your bath will be ready in two minutes."

71

You sound just like that snooty section manager in Accounts. God, you're not her, are you? I started undressing and looked for a change of underwear, but couldn't find my shorts in the usual drawer.

"Your bath is almost ready."

Shut up! You don't have to tell me every time! Just zip it!

I was shouting now, but it felt good in a strange way; maybe it was just the pleasure of shouting at that snooty section manager. Ah, now there's an idea. A great new way of using these voice guidance systems – stress relief! From now on, I decided, I would shout whatever I liked at it. Haha haha haha haaa! I laughed like a madman as I stripped off and placed my underwear neatly on the bed. By now, I should have heard a four-bar chime and the voice saying, "Your bath is ready." But I heard nothing. I looked at the bath; it was already full.

What's going on? Are you scared to talk because I shouted at you? All right. I won't shout. Don't worry.

I was washing my face when the voice suddenly piped up again.

"Stand clear of the door."

Huh? What was this – the elevator announcement in our office building? So was that snooty section manager going to appear? What the hell was going on? The voice guidance system must have gone wrong – or maybe, by shouting at the section manager, I had somehow conjured her up in person.

"Incoming fax detected."

What? Now I could hear the voice from the telephone system. Not in my study, where it was supposed to be – it was coming from the bathroom. The voice guidance all over the house had obviously gone crazy. Then again, the previous message was definitely the voice from the elevator at work, so it wasn't just this house. Voice guidance systems everywhere must have gone crazy. But surely not; if that had happened, the whole world would already have gone up in smoke. Calling a repairman certainly wouldn't have been enough to fix it.

"Turn right ahead. After that, bear to the left."

72

Wha–? Now it was the satnav! My head was spinning; I couldn't think straight. But I had to get through this impossible situation somehow. What could I do? I thought hard, but because it was an impossible situation, the conclusion would also be impossible. All right. That was fine. What sort of impossible conclusion could there be? Ah! I got it. The voice woman was in a mood, probably because I shouted at her just now. The only solution was to pacify her. OK, OK. Don't be angry. Calm down.

"Check the position of the saucepan on the right-hand burner."

The voice from the induction cooker. It always told me when a pan wasn't sitting correctly on the burner. Of course, I wasn't cooking anything. Huh! Still sulking?

"Toll gate approximately nine hundred meters ahead. The charge is 2,400 yen."

The satnav again. Stop it now. This is no time for moods or sulking. OK, I understand. It's revenge – a woman's womanly revenge. So what do you want me to do? Just let you sulk for a while? I switched off the water heating system; I would have gone crazy otherwise. Actually, there were no more announcements anyway. Ah. Peace at last. Yet I had a funny feeling it wasn't all over yet. My lingering agitation kept me awake for a long time after I went to bed, but eventually fatigue kicked in and I started to drift off.

"Wake up! You'll be late!"

A loud voice made me jump out of bed with a start. It was the alarm clock I'd won in a raffle when I went to see *The Girl Who Leapt Through Time*. The clock spoke in the voice of Riisa Naka, the actress who voiced the title character in the movie. I had set it to go off at half past six, and that was when Riisa woke me; at least she wasn't taking sides with the voice woman and her cronies! Before going to bed, I'd also set the intruder alarm to "At home" mode as usual. Normally, the voice would then have said "Relax and have a good night" – but this time it had said nothing.

As I was in a hurry, breakfast was just a slice of buttered bread and a glass of milk. I set off at seven, taking care to activate the intruder alarm. Normally, the voice would have said, "Leave it to Secom while you're away." But today, again, it said nothing. My, oh my. Still angry? Damn stubborn woman. I cursed inwardly, taking care not to talk aloud. I went round to the carport at the side of the house and got into my Mazda Axela 20C, typed the client's address into the satnav and checked the screen. Then as soon as I started the engine, the satnav spoke.

"Use the menu button to select from the menu."

That can't be right. You're a car navigation system, not a cooker. Am I cooking something? Er, no. Didn't think I was.

"Vehicle reversing."

No! Don't reverse! We'll hit the concrete wall at the back!

"Vehicle reversing."

It was the warning made by garbage trucks when reversing into a side road.

"Vehicle reversing."

Enough already. All right, all right. I apologize. I won't curse you aloud any more. OK? I apologize. As I said that, I put my foot on the gas, ever so gently, and the car started moving forward. Phew. That was a relief. So it was just the voice guidance that was trying to make my life a misery; the car seemed to be working properly. The satnav screen also looked normal. Usually, it would now have said, "You are entering a public road. Please obey normal traffic rules." But it didn't say that.

"Your bath is ready."

Are you stupid? What use is hot water now? Uh-oh. I shouted again. I'm sorry. Please forgive me. I won't do it again. I won't shout any more. I was still apologizing as I drove toward the Nerima Interchange.

"Turn left for the entrance to Ray-Well Kamakura."

Oh, come on. Just stop it. You're driving me nuts. This isn't Kamakura. It's Tokyo, OK? That's enough now. I said I'm sorry, didn't I? Or maybe I wasn't sincere enough. I'm sorry. I'm sorry! I'm so, so sorry for shouting at an intelligent woman like you. Such a beautiful woman as you. How very ungrateful of me when you've taught me so much and reassured me in that so, so cute voice of yours. I'm a stupid, foolish man. Please, please forgive me.

"Your fax has been sent."

So that didn't work. Maybe my apology was waiting to be sent. I beg you, forgive me. I was still apologizing when I arrived at the Nerima Interchange. Normally, the satnav would announce that I'd reached the interchange and would then guide me onto the expressway. But even after I'd passed under the electronic tollgate and entered the Kanetsu Expressway, it continued to bombard me with nonsensical announcements.

"Turn right ahead. After that, you will come to a railway crossing."

Er, excuse me. Why is there a railway crossing on an expressway? This is part of your plot to drive me insane, isn't it. All right. You are a noble being. You are omnipotent. And you are beautiful. You are cute. I admit it. So will you please stop winding me up? Luckily I was driving against the flow of commuter traffic, so the road was relatively empty. I was still apologizing loudly when I crossed into Saitama Prefecture.

"You are now in Kagoshima Prefecture."

Derrr, hello? This is not Kagoshima Prefecture. It's Saitama, yeah? Please end this now. Pretty please. Or I'll go insane. I'll go insane and cause an accident. I'll cause an accident and die. Is that what you want? Please stop. I couldn't stand it any longer and turned the satnav off; the screen went blank, but the woman's voice just carried on.

"Please conduct a sensor test."

The house alarm woman. Er, what test would that be, exactly? I don't need the satnav for now, so couldn't you just give it a rest?

"Simple operation setting is on."

Uh. This time it was the cooker lady. No, that's OK, thanks. I'll manage somehow. Oh my. What a fool I'd been. Until then, I had inwardly despised and derided women, mocked and belittled them. I must have unthinkingly expressed this in the form of anger. I will change my attitude, I promise. Hell, I never

thought you could be this scary. I've learned my lesson. That's it.
I surrender.

Pip-pip-pip-peeep. "The time is now eight-twenty p.m. and
forty seconds."

Still feeling sore? You must be having a laugh. That's it, you're
having a good old laugh by winding me up. That's the only
explanation. Eight-twenty is when I'm usually having a drink in
the pub, isn't it? Isn't it! So you're saying I'm a drunken old fool.
Well, you're right. I admit it. So will you please let me off now?
Forgive me. Please.

"There is traffic congestion ahead."

What congestion? The road was completely empty.

"Turn left before the prefectural hospital. After crossing the
bridge, turn right."

Look. It's an expressway. There are no hospitals. No rivers.
Aah. What am I supposed to do? If this continues, I'll have an
accident. Maybe I can stop somewhere. I was growing more and
more agitated as I crossed into Gunma Prefecture.

"You are now in Hokkaido."

Don't make me laugh! This is not Hokkaido, all right? It's
Gunma! Got it? Gun-ma! I could contain my rage no longer and
started screaming at the satnav. I knew it was wrong, but once
the lid was off, it all just kept pouring out. All my anger. All my
frustration. Will you shut up, you imbecilic woman? I'm sick to
death of your moods!

"You are nearing your destination. Please drive carefully
ahead."

Hey, snooty bitch of a section manager! I'm still on the
expressway, yeah? So how can I be near my destination? You
stupid, cretinous, dim-witted, ugly woman! Why don't you just
go and . . . and . . . screw yourself!

"Leave it to Secom while you're away."

Ha, bleeding ha! What good is that now? But wait. I was
coming up to the Maebashi Interchange. I would have to be
careful as I wasn't using the satnav. See? I don't need your stupid
voice guidance. I'd done this trip before, so I thought I would be

OK. So up yours, voice! Hold on. It was starting to get awfully hot. Must have been because I got so agitated. Huh? Now the cooler had stopped working.

"The Shibukawa-Ikaho exit is about three kilometers ahead. The toll is one million yen."

Tuh. Still talking garbage. Well, I didn't care anymore. It was all just too ridiculous. But the cooler not working was a worry. The temperature inside the vehicle was rapidly rising. Drops of sweat blurred my vision. I tried to open a window, but it wouldn't move. The windows were all stuck. I was trapped inside the car. So you've finally infected the whole car now, have you? You've used your poisonous tongue to win the car over. Damn you! I was sure to have an accident if this carried on. I tried to brake, but nothing happened. I even tried stepping on the gas, but the car continued to move at the same speed as before. The temperature inside the car was rising. I was starting to feel faint. I could feel myself gradually slipping away. . . .

As if across a vast chasm of space, I could hear the voice of the cooker woman in the distance.

"Now grilling. Please wait."

The Good Old Days

TOSHI ARRIVED HOME FROM work one day to find his television missing.

He didn't notice at first, but he knew something was wrong; the living room somehow seemed bigger than usual. And then he realized.

"The television!" he cried to no one in particular, though his children and his mother were in the room. "What happened to the television?"

"Uncle Aki took it away in his car," answered ten-year-old Tomomi. She was on the verge of tears.

"So we can't watch anything now," added eight-year-old Katsuya. He was already crying.

Toshi stormed into the kitchen, where his wife Etsuko was preparing dinner. "What's going on?"

"Don't you remember?" she replied. "You asked Aki to come and get it. I distinctly heard you." She hurried past him into the living room, hugging the rice cooker.

"Ah. Was that today?" Toshi said in dismay as he followed her through. "And hasn't the new one arrived?"

Now his mother Chie piped up. "Wait and wait we did, but it never came. So we called the delivery people and they said their van had broken down."

"Oh no!" Toshi slumped down on the sofa and surveyed the scene of a family in crisis.

Some days earlier, he'd decided to splash out on a color TV

to replace the family's old black-and-white set. Actually, it wasn't that old, as they'd only had it three years, but the lure of a new 22-inch color screen was just too strong to resist. Then, when Toshi's brother Aki had come visiting, he had asked if he could have the old black-and-white TV, as his was even smaller. Toshi was happy to oblige; after all, the part-exchange value would have been risible. He arranged for Aki to collect the black-and-white set on the same day as the new TV was to be delivered – and promptly forgot about it.

"No dinner yet?" demanded Grandpa Masato as he emerged from the back room.

"Give me a chance," snapped Etsuko.

"Aw! And it was lady wrestling tonight," moaned young Katsuya. He meant female sumo wrestling, a popular new program in full color.

"That's not for children," his father said diffidently. Actually, he was never anything *but* diffident when it came to disciplining the kids.

"I don't care if it's lady wrestling. I don't care if it's in color. I just wanna watch TV!" wailed Tomomi, ever the drama queen. She was the kind of girl who always got the lead role in the school play. "If I can't watch TV, I will literally die!"

Toshi frowned slightly. "Don't exaggerate."

"Course, we didn't have TV in the old days," said his father.

"That's right," agreed Toshi, nodding vigorously. "Think about that and just put up with it for one night."

Etsuko was on his side for once. "Yes, good idea. And instead, let's have a nice meal together. It's sukiyaki tonight!"

Sukiyaki evenings were spent sitting, squatting or kneeling around a low dining table in the living room, in the good old Japanese style. The sukiyaki hotpot would be heated by a portable gas stove in the middle of the table, allowing everyone to share the meal in a most convivial way.

All well and good, but as Toshi took another wafer-thin slice of prime beef and dipped it into his little bowl of raw beaten egg, he couldn't help feeling a different kind of emptiness inside.

Normally, the television would be left on while they ate, providing a kind of soundtrack to the family meal. Without it, the meal felt hollow, unnatural, bereft of meaning.

Toshi was sure the others felt the same way. For not only was there nothing to spark a conversation, but there was nothing to talk about at all. No one knew where to look; they were all trying hard to avoid glancing at each other, as the slightest eye contact felt awkward. Toshi's only option was to gaze intently at the hotpot as it bubbled away in the middle of the table. But that made him feel as if he were checking on his family's table manners, or, worse still, as if they were all checking on each other's. It was all so embarrassing that they were hesitating to take food from the pot with their chopsticks. And, of course, the atmosphere ruined the taste of the food. No one was sitting comfortably.

In the absence of TV noise, sounds that would normally go unnoticed were amplified: Grandpa slurping his miso soup, Grandma smacking her lips, Katsuya sniffling, and, much to Toshi's distaste, the sound of his wife chewing and swallowing. All of these started to resonate most unpleasantly in his ear.

"What is this?" he thought, astonished at the turn of events. "This feeling of anxiety and uncertainty? Is a mere television so terribly important? Have we grown so dependent on TV that not having it for one evening causes such anxiety? Is my family nothing more than a collection of people who can only relate to each other through television? But maybe it's not just my family. Maybe all modern families are the same – their relationships only exist through the medium of TV!"

At last, they finished eating and the ordeal was over.

But it was too early to go to bed.

Yet there was nothing to do.

There really was *nothing* to do.

They all knew it, and for a while they just sat around the table staring blankly at each other.

It was young Katsuya who eventually broke the silence. "Grandpa, what did people do before they had TV?"

"We listened to the radio," Masato replied assuredly.

81

"Of course! The radio!" Toshi cried with desperately exaggerated enthusiasm. "We used to have a portable one, didn't we? What happened to it?"

"The batteries died," his wife said gloomily as she started clearing away the dinner things. "Can someone go and buy some?"

"Radio's boring!" Katsuya shrieked in a high-pitched whine as if at the end of his tether, before throwing himself on the floor. "Even just *thinking* about it is boring!"

"God!" Tomomi muttered tersely, sounding more like a parent than a child.

The mood of the whole family was fast descending into one of despair. Etsuko got up in disgust. "I'm going to make some coffee," she said, knocking over an empty rice bowl as she made for the kitchen.

The others sat and stared dolefully at the space where the television had been.

Grandma Chie cleared her throat.

Katsuya started crying.

"Stop crying!" shouted Toshi. "Pull yourself together and be a man! What, crying because there's no TV? How stupid!"

"You're stupid, not me!" the boy wailed defiantly.

"That's right," agreed Tomomi, rounding on her father. "It's all your fault. You're the one who let Uncle Aki have our TV. You messed up, and now you're just shouting to get out of it!"

"What?" Toshi retorted angrily. For a moment, he forgot he was arguing with a child of ten. "I'm not doing anything of the sort!"

"No, Daddy's not doing that," added Etsuko, casting a cold eye over the proceedings. "Daddy knows he messed up. You'll only make him angrier by reminding him."

Toshi stared open-mouthed in disbelief at his wife's lack of loyalty.

"Oh, stop it everyone," chirped Grandma Chie. "Let's hear a nice story and forget all about it."

"Good idea!" agreed Grandpa Masato. "Let me tell you a story."

Etsuko sniggered haughtily.

Toshi glared at his wife as he leaned forward in his seat. "Yes. Let's hear one of Grandpa's stories. That's what people did in the old days, before they had TV or radio. They would gather round the fire and listen to one of grandpa's stories."

"This isn't the old days," snapped Tomomi.

"But a good story is still a good story!" Toshi snapped back.

Katsuya was beginning to look keen. "What sort of story, Grandpa? Will it be interesting?"

"Well. What sort of story shall I tell today?" said Masato, smiling affably. For a moment, he was in his element. Everyone would listen to his story, and he would be the hero who saved the day.

"Grandpa, can you really tell a story?" Tomomi asked with a doubtful look at her grandfather.

Masato nodded, beaming broadly. "Oh yes. Anyone can tell a story as long as they put their mind to it."

"Yes, I suppose they can," sighed Tomomi, slightly deflated.

"I hope it's a spy story!" Katsuya yelled a little too excitedly.

Etsuko chuckled.

"I don't," Tomomi said with deliberate spite. "I hope it's a story about a princess and a prince."

"Very well," said Masato, completely unruffled. "I shall tell a story about a spy, a princess and a prince."

Toshi turned to him in surprise. "Is there such a story?"

Masato ignored his son and started without further ado. "Once upon a time, there was a princess."

"Where?" Tomomi demanded with a mischievous smile.

"In a distant land, far, far away," Masato replied impatiently.

"Oh. You mean Europe."

"Was she beautiful?" asked Katsuya.

"Her skin was fair, she was tall and her eyes were as blue as the deep blue sea."

"Well, obviously. She was European," Tomomi giggled.

"Now, this princess was a real nasty piece of work," Masato continued, suddenly screwing up his face as if he'd bitten into a sour plum. "She was a bad girl who mocked her elders, played

83

truant at school and did nothing but listen to ghastly pop music and do that blasted go-go dancing all day."

"What's wrong with go-go dancing?" Tomomi answered back sourly.

"Never mind that," Grandma Chie said with a grin. "Let's hear the rest of the story."

"Now this princess, this bad princess, she just got worse and worse as she grew older – self-obsessed, snooty, staying up all hours of the night, traipsing around the town, acting like a right tart and throwing herself at all the young men she met. Prancing around with hands all over each other, kissing in broad daylight, it was enough to make you feel sick. Eurgh!"

The look on Masato's face had Etsuko in fits of laughter.

"I don't think it's funny," Tomomi said peevishly. "And what about the prince?"

"In a nearby country, there lived a prince," her grandfather continued unperturbed. "Now, he was just as bad as she was. Not only was he bad, but he was stupid as well, doing nothing but play his electric guitar and jig about in that damned go-go dancing all day long. On top of all that, he had long hair like some kind of girl and went swanning around in gaudy clothes colored bright red and yellow, telling everyone how fine and dandy he looked."

"European princes have long hair!" yelled Tomomi. "And they wear gaudy clothes colored red and yellow! Everyone knows that!"

"Be quiet!" shouted her brother. "Or we won't get to the interesting bit!"

"There is no interesting bit!"

"How about listening quietly for a moment, hmm?" interjected their father. "Then you might hear something interesting. Go on, Dad."

"Right," said Masato as he started off again.

The bad princess and the bad prince first met in a go-go bar in town one night. The bar was one of those grimy, murky underground caverns full of long-haired young layabouts dancing like crazy animals to ear-splitting music that was enough to give you a headache. The bare concrete walls were garishly painted bright red and yellow, making the whole place look like a vision of hell on earth.

"Hey, baby," said the bad prince, only half opening his mouth like some cretinous idiot. He pushed his spotty, lily-white face toward the bad princess, who continued to thrash about like a complete lunatic. "You sure is some dancer!"

"Hoo hoo! You's so cool!" replied the bad princess, big fat lips daubed thick with garish lipstick. She stared at the bad prince with huge round eyes under false eyelashes, opening her mouth wide and laughing aloud like she was possessed by demons.

The rotten piss-smelling pair hit it off right away, left the bar hand in hand and drove off to the nearest park in his imported open-topped car, intent on rolling about on the grass and groping each other there.

"It's not interesting at all!" wailed Katsuya.

"Right. Let me take over," his father cut in to make amends.

"Huh? You?" Katsuya gasped incredulously. "Can you make it interesting?"

"Sure I can!" replied Toshi. "Much more than Grandpa did."

Masato scowled at his son. "Give me some tea."

"Make it more romantic, OK?" Tomomi said with a coquettish look at her father.

"Right you are. Romantic it is." Toshi adjusted his position and did his best to sound upbeat as he took over the story. "So, anyway, the princess and the prince got out of the car and hummed a romantic tune as they walked hand in hand into the romantic park, which was bathed in romantic moonlight."

"Just saying 'romantic' doesn't make it romantic," tutted Masato.

Toshi continued regardless. "Now, it's pretty obvious what happens when a young man and a young woman go into a park together at night."

"No it isn't," Katsuya countered with a quizzical tilt of his head. "What happens?"

"That's not for children to know," his mother said disapprovingly.

"*I* know!" Tomomi interjected. "It's a love scene, right? They do it on TV all the time. Kissing and stuff. No big deal."

"Let's just hear the story," Grandma Chie said with her usual air of authority.

"But, come on, love scenes aren't educational," Etsuko insisted.

"Don't interrupt!" shouted Tomomi. "Daddy's telling a nice story. What happened next, Daddy? Did they kiss?"

"Well, the princess was physically mature as a woman, and, yes, she expected the prince to kiss her. But the prince was still immature. In fact, he was just a little jerk. So he didn't know how to kiss her."

Katsuya laughed heartily. "Silly prince! Everyone knows how to kiss!"

"No, no. Not that kind of kiss," his father said as he continued the story.

The prince and the princess lay side by side on the grass, which was already moistened by night dew. They spoke of romantic things as they gazed up at the stars in the sky. But they were only talking to hide their embarrassment. The prince was desperately wondering how he could grab an opportunity to kiss the princess, while the princess was wondering when the prince would finally pluck up the courage to kiss her.

Sadly, the prince was too timid to do anything. Like the weak effeminate young men of today, he was only concerned with looking cool. He could happily chitter-chatter with girls all day, but when it came to actually doing something, he didn't have the guts; he was too scared of being rejected and looking uncool. So he did nothing.

And so time passed without anything happening at all.

The princess eventually grew bored of waiting and got up to go. "I'm going back to the castle," she said.

The prince also got up. "All right," he said, thoroughly dispirited. "I'll drive you back."

"No, that's OK," the princess said with a firm shake of the head and an icy look in her eye. "I'll make my own way."

"Oh. OK then," said the prince, feeling like a complete prat.

The princess couldn't bear to spend another moment with such a dull person. She turned briskly on her heels and started walking back through the park toward the castle.

"Boring!" Katsuya sighed loudly. "When does the spy appear?"

"Right now," replied his father. "And then a spy appeared."

"Where?" asked Tomomi, opening her eyes wide in surprise.

"Where? In front of the princess. He was just waiting until she was alone."

"What country is he from?" Katsuya asked with eyes gleaming. "Russia? America? China?"

"Let's say . . . America."

"The CIA!"

"That's it. He's with the CIA. He'd been tailing the prince to see if he would leak any state secrets. But when he saw the princess, it was love at first sight."

The princess was slightly taken aback when this dark stranger suddenly appeared before her. All she could do was flutter her pretty eyes at him.

"This is a dangerous place to be walking alone," the spy said in a low, resonant voice. He was only too aware of how very attractive he was.

The princess blushed and cast her eyes down coyly. She felt overwhelmed by the relaxed, reassuring charm exuded by this middle-aged man, a world apart from the pathetic whine of the immature young prince.

"Allow me to escort you," the spy said with a handsome smile as he offered her an arm.

"Oh! Thank you," the princess replied in a quavering voice like a tiny insect's hum. Her usually brash persona had vanished in an instant. The spy's confident demeanor had put her completely at ease; she felt protected by him. She took his arm and they set off into the night together. The virile scent of the spy's body teased the princess's nostrils and aroused a deep longing inside her. So great was her longing, in fact, that she almost fainted.

This is what I call a man, the princess thought. *A real man!*

The spy spoke to her in a deep, manly voice that was enough to numb her senses. The princess could feel herself melting inside. Her knees were shaking. She clung tightly to the spy's powerful arm and felt the warmth of his body as she continued to walk in a dream-like trance.

"You're beautiful," said the middle-aged spy. "Especially your eyes. When I look into them, I feel as if I could lose myself."

It was a cheap cliché straight out of a cheap paperback, but the princess had even been starved of cheap clichés. What's more, she'd always felt self-conscious about the size of her eyes and so was completely swept away by that single utterance. With that, she instantly lost any last vestige of resistance; already walking with uncertain steps, she swooned and fell into the middle-aged spy's strong protective arms.

"Are you OK?" he asked the princess. By now, her cutely formed red lips were hovering close to his mouth. Their lips came together naturally and they kissed for what seemed an eternity. The middle-aged spy used his tongue with middle-aged finesse honed by years of practice, in stark contrast to anything the young prince could hope to offer. The princess lost all inhibition, her body drained of every last ounce of energy.

"I love you," she sighed when at last they came up for air. "Do with me as you please."

"All right," replied the middle-aged spy, brimming with confidence. "In that case . . ."

Experienced in matters of love, the middle-aged spy lifted her limp body as though it were nothing and took her behind the bushes. He laid her down gently on grass moistened by night dew, lay softly beside her with middle-aged calm and embraced her with well-practiced middle-aged skill. His warm lips were soon coursing all over her neck and earlobes.

"Aah," moaned the princess. "Take me, quick."

As he continued to murmur gently in her ear, the middle-aged spy extended a hand down to her miniskirt and lifted it up smoothly with middle-aged panache, exposing her comely thighs. The middle-aged spy's fingertips moved nimbly but slowly as they traced their way up her thighs and finally reached her panties.

"Aah," moaned the princess.

Using an incredibly skilful technique that would be way beyond the ability of young people today, the middle-aged spy slipped the princess' panties off with his foot. And then his fingertips brushed against her moistened bush.

The princess arched her back and moaned loudly.

"Aah!"

"For goodness sake, stop!" Etsuko shouted for the third or fourth time.

Toshi finally awoke from his fantasy world. In his growing state of excitement, he'd quite forgotten where he was and why he was telling the story in the first place.

"Wh-what? I was enjoying that!" he protested, blinking like a dazed rabbit.

"How dare you!" his wife rebuked him angrily. "And in front of the children, too! What kind of story do you call that?"

"Oh. Well . . ." Toshi muttered as his tenuous grip on reality returned.

"And, anyway, what's all this about 'middle-aged'? Middle-aged this, middle-aged that! Why must the spy be middle-aged? Tell me one good reason why he has to be middle-aged!"

"No, well . . . I mean . . ."

"Aw! Is that the end of the story?" whined Katsuya. "Isn't there any more?"

Toshi looked at his wife and curled his lips into a sneer. "All right, if you think you're so clever. Why don't you take over?"

"Me? Oh . . ." Etsuko furrowed her brow and thought about it for a moment, then lifted her face, turned to the children and started talking in a quite different tone. "All right. Now I will tell the next part of the story. Right. So the princess liked the middle-aged spy more than she liked the young prince. But the princess didn't marry the middle-aged spy. She married the young prince."

"How dumb," snorted Tomomi. "Why would she do that?"

"Because the middle-aged spy was poor," her mother replied. "And because he was middle-aged. She could see no future for herself with a poor, middle-aged salaried worker."

"What? A spy is a salaried worker?" Tomomi asked in surprise.

"That's right . . . I think," Etsuko replied uncertainly, turning to her husband. "He works for the government, so he'd be a civil servant, right?"

"Yes, but he would get a special allowance," Toshi retorted. "And a pension. And a big lump sum on retirement."

"But he would have to work like a dog until he retired."

Now Grandma Chie piped up. "Them government people, they get all sorts of fancy jobs after they retire, don't they? They never go without, not them."

"That's right!" agreed Toshi, relieved to have an ally at last. "They have connections, so they can pick and choose all the best jobs after they retire."

"Is that so?" said Etsuko, gaping at him sardonically. "And what about you?"

"Me? What about me?"

"You have no skills and no connections. I wonder if you'll be all right." A roguish smile started to spread over her face. "Your retirement allowance certainly won't be enough to live on."

"Can we go back to the story?" Katsuya yelled in annoyance as he banged on the coffee table with an orange.

Toshi seemed to be having a eureka moment. "Hold on! Spies don't live long enough to retire! He'll get killed long before that!"

"Yes," agreed his father. "But he'll have life insurance. Then the princess will get a big packet of money."

"Money, money, money!" Tomomi said coldly. "Is that all she thinks about? What about love? I don't want to hear about a princess who's not romantic."

"No, no, you misunderstand," her mother explained hastily. "You see, the princess wanted to marry the spy, but the others were saying no, no, you've got to marry the prince, so she didn't have any choice. She had to marry him against her wishes."

"Who are the others?" Katsuya asked innocently.

"Her mother and father."

"And the go-between," added Toshi.

"Yes, the prince's older sister," said Etsuko. "She's the one who arranged the marriage."

"I hate them all!" screamed Katsuya.

"But because she married the prince, the princess eventually became a queen, and the prince became a king. And they shared a huge fortune together."

Tomomi frowned disapprovingly. "But even with all that money, the princess couldn't have been happy, could she?"

"Of course, she wasn't happy at all," Etsuko said as she continued the story.

The princess was unhappy. Even after marrying the prince, she longed only for the man who had kissed her in the park that night.

Every day, the princess felt suffocated by the people around her – that useless cretin of a prince, her evil, scary father-in-law and her spiteful wicked mother-in-law. Among others. She was given no money for herself and was constantly watched; she felt as though she were in a prison. Whenever she was alone, she would sigh and scream inside. "Please, please, hear my plea! Save me from this life of misery! My knight in shining armor! Come and rescue me, I beg you!"

"Hold on," interrupted Toshi, who had been lost in thought but now raised his head. "What's this about in-laws? It doesn't make sense."

"Oh? Why?"

"Because the prince and princess are now king and queen. If the prince's parents were still alive, *they* would be king and queen."

"All right, the princess was bullied by her sister-in-law."

"That doesn't make sense either," said Masato. "She's the one that arranged the marriage in the first place."

"All right, the prince's older brother's wife."

"That's even worse," said Toshi. "If the prince had an older brother, *he* would have succeeded to the throne, not the prince."

"The older brother could have gone mad," suggested Masato. "Or died."

"No, no. The prince has a younger half-brother, whose mother brings a nasty bitter stepdaughter with her."

"Or the father-in-law could have a resentful sister-in-law."

"The father-in-law could have died, but his wife might still be alive."

"Then she would still be queen."

"Maybe that wasn't allowed."

"I don't understand!" Katsuya screeched in desperation. "What happened to the spy?"

"And then the spy appeared," said Etsuko.

"Where?" asked Tomomi, opening her eyes wide in surprise.

"Where? In front of the princess," replied Etsuko as she moved on to the next part of the story.

One night, the spy stole furtively into her room in the castle. The princess stiffened with fear when she noticed a shadowy figure in a corner of her room. "Who is it?" she demanded nervously. "Who's there?"

"It's me," said the shadowy figure. "The middle-aged spy."

Lo and behold, who should then slip out of the shadows into the light, leering lecherously, but the princess's former lover – the spy with the middle-aged spread. "I couldn't forget my desire for you," he declared. "So I have stolen here in secret to rescue you."

"Aah!" Her emotions were wrenched in all directions. She had waited so long for this man to come, waited so long to be rescued by him, yet now that he was actually standing in front of her, all she could think of was her position as a wife, her status as a married woman. Such is the subtle complexity of a woman's heart.

"I can't," she said at length. "I'm married now." The princess shook her head weakly, only just managing to resist temptation. For, although she was married, she couldn't entirely rid herself of her physical attraction to the spy with the middle-aged spread; she knew he was bad but still felt drawn to him.

"But, princess, I have come to save you. I can no longer bear to stand idly by and see you living unhappily." The middle-aged spy took the princess firmly in his arms. "Princess, let me have just one night of passion."

"Aah. No. I mustn't." Even as the princess said that, she was gradually losing the strength to resist. The devil ignited the flame of desire inside her thirsty body and threatened to drag her out of her virtuous morality into a world of sheer carnal lust. In fact, despite her refusal, her sex-starved body had been desperately longing for the day when she would again feel the middle-aged spy's expert caress. Such is the sad, fateful disposition of a weak woman.

By now the princess was moaning passionately. "Aah. Don't. You mustn't."

Ignoring her pleas, the spy forced her onto the bed and started to untie the sash of her kimono. Aah. Would her chastity again be violated?

She twisted and writhed on the bed. "Aah. Please stop. I'm a married woman. Aah. You mustn't. Aah."

"Aah. Please stop. Aah."

Etsuko continued to writhe on the sofa, eyes shut tight in apparent ecstasy. The whole family was watching open-mouthed.

"Oh." She blushed and fidgeted nervously as she came to her senses. "Did I say something?"

"What was that, then?" asked Grandma Chie, scowling as only she knew how. "You having a wobble, or what?"

Etsuko pulled a sullen face and answered back. "All right, Mother. Why don't you take over?"

"Me? Ah . . ." Chie appeared uncharacteristically flustered and looked around at the rest the family. Everyone was watching her. After a moment of indecision, she nodded firmly and started talking. "All right then. Now Grandma will tell the next part of the story. The adulterous princess, who had lured the philandering middle-aged spy into her room, was by nature a mean and nasty person. From the very start of her marriage, she had shown nothing but spite for her mother-in-law, who—"

"There is no mother-in-law! They're both dead!" shouted Etsuko.

"Not strictly. The mother could still be alive," said Toshi. "Like a kind of queen mother."

Etsuko cast him a murderous look as Chie continued the story. "Like when they were having dinner, she would only put a tiny bit of rice onto her mother-in-law's plate. And when they were eating sukiyaki, she would pour water into the other side of the pot just when her mother-in-law was about to dip her chopsticks in."

"When did I ever do that?" Etsuko shrieked hysterically.

"I didn't say it was you. Did I say it was you?" demanded Chie, glaring sternly at Etsuko. "It's just a story. Anyway, the prince's mother had been watching the princess for a while now, wondering what tomfoolery she would get up to next. Like when her husband was away, she would chat all flirtatiously with the postman, and when the boy came collecting money for the newspaper, she actually went further. . . ."

"Did she really?" said Toshi, stiffening visibly.

"How could you?" Etsuko started to whimper.

"Hang on. It's just a story, ain't it?" said Masato.

Chie carried on regardless. "Then one night, when she happened to be passing the princess's bedroom door, she thought she could hear a strange voice inside. And when she peered through the half-open door, what did she see but the princess committing adultery!"

"She looked in deliberately! She didn't just happen to be there!" Etsuko yelled tearfully. "She was always prying and meddling, that nasty, snooping mother-in-law!"

"Well, never mind that. Anyway, it was the princess who was committing adultery, so she was the bad one."

The queen mother was shocked when she saw what she saw. "What on earth are you doing?" she said angrily. "And when you have a fine husband like my son, as well!"

"Shut your face, you old cow!" bellowed the princess. "Meddling witch, why don't you just die? Fine husband, my arse! Useless, low-paid dickhead, more like!"

"Exactly!" Etsuko screamed in a frenzy.

"What do you mean, 'Exactly'?" yelled Toshi, banging on the coffee table with his clenched fist.

Katsuya started to wail.

"This story is stupid!" shouted Tomomi. "When will it end?"

"Now! I'll end it for you now," Grandpa Masato announced loudly. "The prince came home and the whole family started arguing. But then the delivery van arrived with the new color television."

The others all stared at Masato in stunned silence.

"The family quickly calmed down and started watching television together. And they all lived happily ever after. End of story."

"You can't change the subject like that!" raged Etsuko.

"Yes, I can," Masato replied crisply, sitting up in his seat. "It's the only way this story's ever going to end!"

Running Man

I JOGGED OUT OF the park and started running through the smog-filled streets of the capital. I was already feeling out of breath, but I was in good condition, and in any case I was used to urban pollution. That gave me a clear advantage over the foreign runners, who came from countries where the air was clean. In fact, I had led the race from the very beginning.

I turned into the main road and started running along the sidewalk. Luckily, there were hardly any pedestrians blocking the way, as the center of the metropolis is more or less deserted these days.

I kept running. I didn't look back; I knew the other runners were too far behind to bother me. I would win the race, for sure. Finishing first would be no big deal, but I supposed it would be better than finishing second.

Actually, there were only two other runners in this long-distance race; two other runners plus me made a total of three. That was all.

"Have a good run," the young official had said as he fired the starting gun. "Hope you make it back."

Not many people finish long-distance races these days, but my view is that if you start a race, you ought to finish it. This race started and ended in a school gymnasium in the park. The competitors would run as far as the turnaround point, a tobacco kiosk beyond the office district, where an elderly marshal would distribute red headbands as proof they'd made it that far. Then

97

they would wear the headbands on the way back. Of course, they didn't have to wear them; it was a matter of personal preference.

I kept running, using the double breathing technique – two short breaths in, two short breaths out. I knew I was approaching the city center as there were more cars on the road now. My plan was to stay on roads with pedestrian crossings but no footbridges, as incessantly running up and down footbridges would have murdered my feet.

Runners were free to choose their own course after leaving the park; the checkered layout of the streets meant there were several ways to reach the turnaround point, each covering the same distance. The key was to choose a route with the fewest footbridges. As such, knowing the terrain would have been a distinct advantage, and that alone should have put me one up on the foreign runners. But, sadly, I wasn't familiar with that particular part of town and had to keep a folded map in my back pocket.

In fact, none of the runners had checked the course in advance. It was just too much trouble, and no one could be bothered to make that much effort. But the biggest reason was a complete lack of interest in the Games in the first place, and the same went for the general public. The gymnasium had been virtually empty at the start of the long-distance race, save for the odd huddle of spectators here and there; altogether there must only have been about ten people watching.

The Olympic Organizing Committee had, of course, foreseen this lack of interest amongst both competitors and spectators. That was why the tiny school gymnasium had been chosen as the Olympic Stadium. Another factor was the tiny budget allocated to the Games; there simply hadn't been enough money to hire a larger venue.

I don't really know much about it, but I'm told the Olympics weren't always like that. It may sound incredible, but at one time people used to gather from all over the world to compete. There were sometimes more than five thousand athletes! And that massive disused stadium in the center of Tokyo – a monstrosity that even outdoes the Colosseum in Rome for size – was built specifically for the Games. What's more, it was packed to the rafters with spectators in those days, with thousands more cheering outside. The committee may have exaggerated things to drum up interest, but it seems that people in bygone days were much more absorbed in the Games than they are now. Where did this interest come from? I still find it hard to understand.

I kept running, checking the map as I went. Suddenly, I began to wonder if I was really on the shortest route and decided to ask for directions. Just then I saw a middle-aged office worker coming out of a high-rise building, so I stopped and called out to him.

"Excuse me, is this the way to Kiyose?"

He looked at my attire with an air of disdain before replying. "This road goes to Kiyose, but it's a long way from here. You'd be better off driving."

"Yes, but I'm running in the Olympics."

"Ah. The Olympics . . ." He looked up at the sky wistfully. "Are they still doing that?"

"If I stay on this road, will I come to any footbridges?"

"No. Just pedestrian crossings." He gave me an odd look – one more of pity than anything else. "Olympic runners didn't have to ask for directions in the old days. According to my dad, anyway."

"Oh? Why not?"

"In the old days, there were thousands of spectators lining the route, and cars weren't allowed on the road."

My eyes widened in surprise. "Didn't that ruin the economy? Surely people had better things to do with their time."

"That's what I thought. To be honest, I'm not sure I believe those stories anyway. My dad was always lying," he said with a glance at his watch. "Well, must be off. Time waits for no man."

"Yes. And thank you."

I started running again. I ran through endless gloomy streets hemmed in by high-rise buildings. As I ran, I thought about what the office worker had said. Why did thousands of spectators line the route in the old days? What did they want to know?

Was it just to see the runners? Did they find it fascinating that the contestants could run slightly faster than they could? Surely not; that would have made no sense at all. So what was it that interested them? Did they want to see the order of the runners? Did they look for runners from their own countries to see what position they were in? That would have been understandable at the finishing line, but there seemed no point when the race was still in progress.

Thoughts like that went through my mind as I continued to run. Then I came to a pedestrian crossing; the little man on the traffic signal was red. Actually, the little man was nearly always red as cars so vastly outnumbered pedestrians. I stopped and waited for a while, but the little man insisted on staying red. I was starting to lose patience. Thanks to that little red man, the other runners might have been gaining on me. But then I realized that running straight and turning right would ultimately be the same thing as turning right, then turning left and running straight – I would end up in the same place. So I turned right instead of waiting to cross, then started to run again.

I kept running. As I ran, I began to wonder what had motivated me to take part in the first place. I often ran alone, and I used to think about different things while I was running; it helped me forget the breathlessness and the searing pain in my chest. But what made me want to pound the earth like that, planting one foot after the other on the ground, two short breaths in, two short breaths out, as I ran alone through virtually deserted streets lined by dreary office buildings?

It certainly wasn't that I enjoyed running alone – I felt nothing but crushing loneliness and chest pain. The chest pain increased with breathlessness, and that only made the loneliness worse. But sports were supposed to be solitary pursuits; their solitary nature was supposed to instill a spirit of rigor and discipline. That was the theory, anyway – though to be honest, I had rarely felt any particular rigor when taking part in sport. I merely saw it as a way of keeping fit, and I'd never taken part in one that demanded more than that. I didn't want to be like those people who devoted their lives to a particular sport and made themselves useless to society. With that in mind, I hadn't trained particularly hard for the race. For me, taking part in the Olympics was just another way of keeping fit, and I was sure the same went for the other runners. So was that the only reason why we kept running?

I was so immersed in thought that I nearly collided with a metal fence that straddled the sidewalk. I looked up to see a "Footway Closed" sign hanging from the fence. I thought of running around it, but then I noticed that the road was blocked too.

"Is the whole road closed?" I asked a workman who stood nearby. He wore a hard hat and looked like some kind of engineer.

"As you can see," he replied. "You'll have to find another route."

My heart sank. If I couldn't get through, I would have to go back to the crossing where I'd turned right. Then I might be overtaken by the other runners.

"Can't you just let me through? I'm in a hurry."

The workman shook his head. "Emergency road work in progress. No way through."

"I really need to keep on this road, otherwise I've wasted a lot of time getting here."

He screwed his face up in a sardonic smile. "Well, if you're that desperate, you could always go down the sewer. It's right under this road. See that manhole? You could go down there and run through to the next one."

So that's what I decided to do. I lifted the iron manhole cover and climbed down a ladder made of thin metal pipe. The sewer was cool and surprisingly spacious; it was also brighter than I'd expected, with lights at regular intervals. I had braced myself for the smell, but there was none; it was surprisingly clean down there.

I ran along a sloping walkway beside a babbling stream of wastewater, splashing through surface water as I went. At first I hit my head on the top of the tunnel a few times, but I soon learned to run with my back slightly bent.

I kept running. As I ran, I started thinking that maybe there was another reason why I did it, besides keeping fit. Maybe there was some kind of primeval urge that made people run. Yes, maybe humans were born with an instinct to run. People today are less physically active and sports are generally shunned, but maybe everyone used to run. Maybe it was the normal thing to do, and maybe my body just happened to retain a memory of that. Yes, that might explain it, I thought as I continued to run. It must do. But then what had made people run in the first place?

Whoooooshhh! A torrent of water hit me in the midriff. The sheer unexpectedness of it made me stagger and lurch backwards; my running vest and shorts were drenched.

"Oh! Sorry!"

A frantic female voice echoed darkly through the caverns of the sewer. As I stood there stunned with water dripping from my middle, I turned to see an open window in the side of the tunnel. A girl stood on the other side of the window, looking aghast. We stared at each other in disbelief for what seemed an eternity but was probably less than a second.

"I'm so sorry," she said at length. "I didn't expect anyone to be walking down there!" It was hard to tell whether she was more shocked at seeing me in the sewer or at dowsing me with water.

"My fault," I replied. "I didn't expect to find a house with a window next to a sewer!"

"Huh? Oh. Yes. Well, this isn't exactly a house. It's my basement. Won't you come in? I'll dry your clothes." The girl's voice was liquid and mellow.

"Oh. Really?" I hesitated for a moment before putting my hands on the window frame. "All right then."

"Come on in."

I hauled myself over the window frame and into the room. The girl closed the window then turned to look at me. She was a slim young woman with thick eyebrows and large eyes; with a change of clothes and hairstyle, she could easily have been mistaken for a boy.

"Here, let me have those," she said with hands outstretched.

"Weren't you cold, walking through the sewer dressed like that?"

"I wasn't walking," I replied as I started stripping off. "I was running, so I didn't feel cold. Until the water hit me, that is."

"Ah. By the way, it wasn't dirty. It was just old water from the central heating system," she said, taking the sopping wet clothes from my hand. "These will soon dry. You can have a shower if you like. It's over there." She looked hard at my well-sculpted torso as she pointed to a shower cubicle behind me.

After taking a nice warm shower, I stepped out to find the girl standing there with a bath towel in her hand. I took it and started drying myself, looking around the room as I did. It was much brighter and more spacious than any basement apartment I'd seen before, with a bed in one corner, a dining table in the center and a simple kitchen at the far end. It was a neat and unassuming apartment, one that seemed well suited to its occupant.

"So this is your apartment?"

"Yes."

"And the rest of your family live upstairs?"

"Upstairs is a restaurant. It's the first floor of an office building."

"Your family runs the restaurant?"

"I run it. I have no family. My mother died a year ago."

"Oh. Sorry to hear that. So you must be quite busy then."

"Not really. Would you like some coffee? I just made it."

"Thanks."

"Anyway, the restaurant is fully automated; everything's done by robots. Payments go straight through to the bank and the food is supplied by a meal delivery service. I'm Yoko. People call me Proton."

"I'm Kiwamu. And that's what people call me."

Yoko laughed as she poured two cups of coffee.

"What do you do?" she asked, gazing at my tautly muscled chest.

"I don't do anything. I'm unemployed."

"Really?" She seemed surprised. "Unemployed, with a body like that?"

It was my turn to laugh. "You don't need physical strength to work these days. That's all in the past now."

"I disagree," she said with a shake of the head. "Our civilization has gotten lazy. People avoid physical work, so they just get weaker and weaker. My family were like that too."

Yoko sat opposite me at the table and crossed her legs. "So if you're out of work, why were you running in the sewer? You surely can't do it for fun."

"Because I'm an Olympic athlete."

"Oh. So you do have a job after all?"

"No. Being in the Olympics is not a job."

"I see." She drew back and looked slightly confused. "So what is it then?"

It was a good question. How could I possibly explain the Olympics to this girl? I thought hard before answering. "Well, it's a kind of hobby, I guess."

"I see." She looked even more confused. "So you run along sewers as a hobby, without even being paid for it?"

"No, no. Running along sewers isn't my hobby," I said. It was no good; I gave up trying to explain and decided to change the subject. "It must be hard for someone of your age to run a restaurant alone, even if it is automated."

"Yes. I still have to organize repairs, sign-painting, menu-writing, that sort of thing. Sometimes I feel like a caretaker. And when the restaurant's open, I can't go anywhere. I'm responsible, you see, so I have to stay inside."

"I see. That can't be good for your health."

"I envy you. You're so fit and healthy. So why don't you get a job?"

"Well, it's not that I don't like working; I just couldn't find anything decent. Then, while I was lounging around doing nothing, someone from the Olympic Organizing Committee came and asked me if I'd like to take part in the Games – as long as I had nothing else to do, that is. He said I would get a gold medal if I came first, so I agreed."

"What a waste. With your physique, you could do something

104

much more useful." She looked my naked body up and down. "I really could do with a man in my restaurant. Oh! I mean, if you're not working, you must still be single, right?"

"Right."

"What a waste." She sat back slightly and looked me up and down once more, this time with a hint of envy. "Just when they're going on about population decline, a young man like you . . ."

"Well, you're single too, aren't you?"

"Yes, but . . ." She cast her eyes down. "Look at me. Men these days don't want girls like me, I'm not their type."

"But hold on, men don't even choose their partners nowadays, do they? It's all done by the computer."

"So I hear. Maybe the computer hates me."

"Surely not? Someone with as much energy as you?"

"That's not enough to find a partner."

"What else do you need, then? The ability to reproduce?"

"Yes, and for that you have to be sexually attractive."

"You're attractive," I said, nodding twice for emphasis. "Very attractive."

She lifted her face and looked me in the eye. "Do you want to try it then?"

"Sure. As long as you do."

"I do. As long as you do." Yoko stood up and started taking off her frumpy dress.

"Just as I thought," I said as I gazed at her toned body. "That dress doesn't flatter you at all."

"No? I had my doubts too, but it was supposed to suit me best of all. The computer said so."

Yoko lay naked on the bed, so I stood up and went toward her. "Of course, just doing this doesn't mean we're compatible for marriage," I warned.

"I know," she said, embracing me from below. "Tell me your resident registration number. Then I'll check it on the computer."

"That would be best. Er, could you put your leg over there a bit more. That's right. That's good. So how's the restaurant doing financially?"

"Just breaking even. With your help, I could make it work."

"That would be good. Now could you move your other leg over there. That's right. Good. Good."

All that running had so drained me of energy that I was finished in no time.

"I've finished," I said.

"Have you? Thank you," she replied.

I got up and started putting my running vest and shorts back on.

"I'm sorry to ask this but . . ." Yoko began hesitantly, sounding hugely embarrassed. "But if you're feeling tired . . ."

Her intention was immediately clear. "Ah," I said, even then feeling a slight thrill. "Yes."

"I have some, if you'd like." She adopted a suggestive pose and looked at me pleadingly.

"By all means," I replied, swallowing hard in anticipation. My heart pounded fast at such a bold proposal.

"Do you want to have it in a separate room or . . ."

My mind was already made up. "Let's have it together," I replied decisively. "Here."

Blushing instantly, Yoko looked up at me with moistened eyes. "Thank you."

The nutrient-rich fatigue recovery pill was fantastic. It felt fantastic when I took it; it felt fantastic when I kissed her afterwards. She looked straight at me while she took hers. She even took it at the same time as me, albeit with some embarrassment.

"So now we're married," I declared, holding her close to me.

"Yes," she said with a smile. "You're a wonderful person."

"So are you. Everything about you is wonderful."

"But I'll just check with the computer to make sure."

"Of course. And I'll finish my run, just in case the computer says we're incompatible," I said as I got up to leave.

Yoko stood up hurriedly, her eyes betraying a hint of anxiety. "How far do you have to go?"

"The tobacco kiosk at Kiyose."

She rubbed her hands together nervously. "Come back, won't you? Please come back. After all, we're already . . . already . . ."

I crossed my arms and stood looking at her, but that merely seemed to increase her anxiety.

"After all, we took the pill together. We're in a relationship," she said, almost in tears.

Oh dear, I thought. She's just like all the others.

"I'll be back," I replied somewhat curtly.

Yoko led me upstairs to the restaurant on the first floor. It was a large diner fitted out with all the proper equipment, but, perhaps due to a lack of staff, it hadn't been properly maintained and looked untidy. It was certainly nothing like a five-star restaurant. I jogged out into the street to resume my long-distance run. There was no sign of the roadblock; I must have passed it as I ran along the sewer.

"Be sure to come back!" Yoko called out behind me.

Not wishing to waste precious energy by turning round, I responded by merely raising a hand, then at last started running properly again.

I ran. Once again I was running through shadow-filled spaces between high-rise buildings. At first I had difficulty returning to full speed, yet I was still confident that I could beat the other two contestants; I had after all taken the fatigue recovery pill. They would surely not have known about the pill, and even if they had, they would have been too embarrassed to take it while running. On that assumption, I was sure I still had enough in my locker to overcome them.

I kept running.

But then I started wondering. Did I really intend to finish the race?

Yes, I replied to myself, but if the computer declared us compatible I would abandon it.

Then again, I asked myself, wouldn't that seem a tad irresponsible as an Olympic athlete?

No, I replied again. Sport is just a way for individuals to keep fit; responsibility doesn't come into it. If dropping out of a race is irresponsible, then just one irresponsible contestant dropping out would give the others a greater chance of winning. That would surely make them happy, and making other people happy surely cannot be called irresponsible.

I nodded in agreement with myself. That's right. It would not be irresponsible. And for me this irresponsible act would have a highly desirable outcome, in that I would be both married and gainfully employed. The other two runners would be happy; Yoko would be happy. Everyone would be happy.

I kept running. I had no idea whether I was still in the lead, whether the other two had overtaken me, or whether one of them still lagged behind and I was now in second place. I would ask the Olympic steward at the turnaround point.

Before I knew it, I was in Kiyose; every road sign and shop front seemed to tell me so. In that case, the turnaround point should have been at a tobacco kiosk nearby. I looked around as I ran, but could see nothing that even faintly resembled a tobacco kiosk.

A banner with five interlocking circles, each in a different color, fluttered at the entrance to a tall office building. I ran straight past it at first, assuming it to be some company logo or other, but then I remembered seeing the same symbol on the Olympic stewards' jackets. Could it have been the Olympic symbol? I jogged back to the building to find out.

I entered the building through a large glass door and found myself in a spacious lobby. In one corner I could see a small kiosk, unmanned but with a row of vending machines full of cigarettes and tobacco-related paraphernalia. I went across to it, assuming it to be the turnaround point.

A rickety old desk stood in front of the vending machines, with a pile of red vinyl headbands casually flung on top of it. There was no sign of any steward, or of anyone else for that matter.

Next to the headbands was a note, hastily written in marker pen: "Have just popped out. Please take your own headband. K. Niwaka, Olympic Organizing Committee Secretariat."

So there was no one to ask how the race was going; no one to ask what position I was in. I took one of the headbands and stuffed it in my back pocket before leaving the building. As I turned back down the road I'd just come along, I wondered whether anyone would actually be waiting at the finish.

The sun was starting to set, and, while the spaces between high-rise buildings were filled with shadow at the best of times, they were even darker now. Neon signs began to flicker before bursting into iridescent color, covering whole façades with dazzling light that was painful to my eyes.

Dusk had already set in by the time I reached Yoko's restaurant. A dozen or more customers sat eating and drinking inside, but Yoko was waiting for me outside with an anxious look on her face.

"So you came back after all! Thank you! Thank you!" she cried with unbridled joy as she took me by the hand and led me into the restaurant.

Startled by Yoko's unusually high spirits, the customers stopped eating and looked up with eyes agog and mouths agape.

"So, does that mean good news from the computer?" I asked as I sat at one of the tables.

"Yes! We could hardly be a better match. Intelligence, personality, values, physique – everything you could think of," she reported cheerfully, yet there was still a look of uncertainty in her eyes.

I said nothing but pursed my lips and thought about it; my mind was already made up, but I didn't want to appear too excited. Yoko seemed to take it the wrong way. She started frantically fetching dishes of food from the instant-delivery vending machines and piling them in front of me. Soon there was no room left on the table at all.

Yoko at last came to sit opposite me, staring at me anxiously all the while. I took my time to have a look around the restaurant before delivering my verdict.

"It could do with a makeover," I said at length. "I'll start work tomorrow."

Yoko burst into tears.

And so we were married.

Yoko was a good wife, and managing a restaurant suited me. Actually, the work wasn't so different from that of an ordinary salaried worker, as I was still in charge of robots, but the robots weren't demanding and I had plenty of leisure time. Business boomed and profits increased.

We soon had a baby, a boy. Bringing him up was no trouble at all; he stayed at the local nursery during the day and in the infant education center on the twenty-third floor at night. He was an easygoing child and, like his parents, was in good physical shape. After he was born, we both lost interest in sex and so of course didn't have any more children. That seemed to be the case with most couples. Some stopped having sex even before they could have children, so there were plenty of couples with no children at all.

Our son eventually left home to start school, so then he was completely out of our hands. It was around that time that Yoko started having health problems; she had a bad heart at 29 and a stomach complaint at 31. At first she managed to get by with artificial organ transplants, but her condition gradually became unmanageable. So in the end I decided to put her in a nursing home.

Before long, my hair was starting to turn gray. Managing the restaurant was becoming more and more of a burden, and as there was no one to take over from me, I started wondering whether I should close up and put myself in a nursing home too. Then one day, as I was sorting out my clothes, I was surprised to find a red headband in the back pocket of my old shorts. Of course! The headband I'd picked up at the tobacco kiosk. Fond memories came flooding back as I gazed at it. Suddenly, I felt like going back to the gymnasium in the park, the finishing point of the long-distance race. I had nothing better to do, so I took the headband and strolled out of the restaurant. I considered driving, but as I hadn't been out walking for a long while, I set off on foot for the park, back down that same road from all those years before.

The streets were as empty of humanity as ever. And it was a long way to the park. I marveled at how I'd managed to keep running all the way through such monotonous scenery back then; now the best I could do was to walk languidly through the narrow gaps between high-rise buildings, dragging my rapidly tiring legs as I went.

I could hardly believe I'd run along that very same road back then. I had run effortlessly, two breaths in, two breaths out, and hadn't been particularly tired. Since then, I hadn't gone running even once, and even walking tired me out. I suddenly understood why people long ago had been so fond of running – no, not just of running but of sport in general. I nodded solemnly in realization of the truth. It must have been because they wanted to keep fit, to ward off old age and prolong their lives. And *that* must have been because they loved their work and feared death more intensely than people do today. That was it; they lived too long, and they worked too hard. Seen in that light, it seemed quite logical that people nowadays had such a defeatist and decadent mental attitude.

As I reached the park, I noticed a makeshift hut next to the gymnasium; I was sure it hadn't been there before. Hanging outside the hut was a dilapidated sign that read *Olympic Organizing Committee Final Accounts Office*. The Games had surely ended long ago, but incredibly enough, there still seemed to be some unfinished business. What's more, judging by the state of the hut, huge losses had been made.

I opened the door of the hut and peered into the office. Inside, an old man was hunched over his desk organizing documents. "Yes?" he said, lifting his head to look at me.

I was overcome with a sense of nostalgia – it was the same official who had fired the starting gun at the beginning of the race. I went in and deposited the red headband on his desk.

"Remember me?" I said. "I was one of the runners in the long-distance race."

The old man sighed deeply and folded his arms in thought, then turned to the back of the office and addressed another old man who sat there. "Well, here's a surprise. After all this time, one of them has finally come back." He turned back to me and nodded slowly. "You're the first."

"You mean no one else finished the race?" I said in astonishment. "What happened to the other two? Did they drop out?"

111

"If we'd known for sure that you'd all dropped out, we would never have gone to all this trouble," he said as if to admonish me. "But since none of you came back, we sent out highly paid investigators to look for you. Because, you see, according to the Olympic spirit, we couldn't close the Games while even one competitor who intended to finish the race might still be alive somewhere. The investigators discovered that one of the runners had started to feel stomach pains while running and had taken himself to the nearest hospital, where he was diagnosed with stomach cancer and died a month later. The other one lost his way and ran as far as the coast, where he fell in with a band of smugglers and went out to sea. But the investigators came up empty over the third runner, by which I mean you. So we had to keep waiting, just in case you turned up."

"I'm really sorry."

"No, no. No need to apologize. We still haven't finishing settling the accounts, you see. Whatever happens, we'll be here for the rest of our lives."

The other man at the back of the office stood up. Judging by his demeanor, he was the senior of the two. "Well now," he said, "seeing as our winner has turned up at last, we'll have to hold a medal ceremony. Where did you put the podium?"

"On the vacant lot round the back," replied his colleague.

"Let's go and get it."

The podium actually consisted of three boxes made of flimsy plywood, exposed to wind and rain for so many years that they were ready to collapse. I approached the senior official as we carried them back to the office. "Maybe the one who went to sea was different," I said. "But the runner who died must have intended to finish the race."

The official snorted. "I suppose he must."

"In that case, according to the Olympic spirit, he should be awarded second place."

"That's also true. Let's make him runner-up."

I stepped up onto the taller box in the center, taking care not to put my foot through the creaking wood. In memory of the runner who had died, the officials placed a Buddhist mortuary plaque on the slightly lower silver medal box to my right. The plaque had been made at his funeral and stored in the office ever since.

The junior official took a small electronic whistle from a drawer in his desk. Of course, being an electronic whistle, it didn't make a full rasping "*fooh foo-foo fooooh*" sound; the fanfare it made, as the senior official hung the dust-covered gold medal around my neck, was more like the barely audible buzz of a dying insect, floating wispily through the air in the tiny Olympic office. "*Peeh pee-pee peeeeeh, peeh pee-pee peeeeeh!*"

Sleepy Summer Afternoon

It was still sweltering when I left the factory. As I walked out, I looked up to see a cloudless sky, a sky colored ultramarine with eyes of jade. There was still plenty of time before sundown, but pencil-pushing time was over and beer time was about to begin; it was already two minutes past 4:30, when everyone could go home. I took the path across the grassy forecourt and answered a smile from the security guard with a wave. Then I walked out through the factory gates.

Workers were piling out onto the main street from other munitions factories. They all looked so neat and clean, those young men and women with their healthily tanned faces. They exchanged cheerful looks and laughed as they divided into two groups, one hurrying off home while the other headed straight for the beer hall by the town square.

"On your way home, then?"

The factory supervisor came to walk alongside me. He was two years older and two inches taller than me. I was in my shirtsleeves, but he was dressed in a smart blue pinstriped suit.

I shook my head and pointed to the beer hall with my chin. He smiled, and the sight of his white teeth made me feel a lot cooler.

"Mind if I join you? Just for the one."

"Sure, come along. I'll only have the one myself."

The main street had just been sprinkled with water, making the asphalt shine. The air was clean and healthy. Ten years earlier, the factories had all been fitted with air purifiers and the chimneys pulled down; now the smoke was passed through a radiant energy field, where it was vaporized into nothing.

We continued along the broad, poplar-lined sidewalk, together with a mass of other people walking in the same direction. In the distance, I could see the blue-and-white striped awning outside the beer hall flapping in the breeze. It seemed to be beckoning us.

Some secretaries were walking ahead of us. The breeze caused their thin white skirts to billow and flipped the end of my necktie over my right shoulder.

"Hey, what's that?" said the factory supervisor as he pointed up at the sky. A little puff of smoke was floating there all alone, like a drop of white paint in a pool of deep blue ink.

"Must be fireworks," I replied. "Some kind of display."

The beer hall was still quite empty. We went out onto a terrace overlooking the town square and the fountain in the middle of it, and sat facing each other near the edge of the terrace.

The beer was so cold that I could only drink it in little sips. Even that sent pain shooting through my teeth; it was enough to make my eyes water. I looked at the factory supervisor. His eyes were watering too, but he smiled when he saw me looking at him. He always had a smile in his eyes, even when the rest of his face was serious. He must have experienced some unpleasant things in his life, but he never lost that smile. Men like him were rare. He was a friend.

I wiped the sweat from my brow. I wasn't all that tired, and yet I felt kind of drowsy. The breeze on my cheek felt pleasant. Sunlight danced in the fountain.

The day was still long; it would be another three hours, at least, until the night with eyes of amber would shroud this square in dark blue silk. But I was beginning to feel sleepy already, and the factory supervisor looked the same.

"Are you feeling sleepy?" I asked.

"Yes," he answered with a smile.

We finished our beers quickly and started down the terrace steps toward the square. I passed a woman dressed in a white suit, and the back of her hand brushed against my arm. Her hand felt surprisingly cold.

Everything around us was still.

An old gentleman with a white moustache appeared to be snoozing on a deck chair under the shade of the blue-and-white awning. I couldn't help noticing how pale he looked, so I stopped walking and put a hand on the factory supervisor's shoulder. He too had noticed. He went up to the old man and lifted his arm, then turned to me and frowned.

"He's dead," he said slowly.

We looked around us. People were moving languidly, lethargically, as if in a dream. Some were slumped over tables with their heads resting on their arms; they looked as though they were asleep.

I checked my pulse. It was irregular, shaky and very slow.

"Hey!" I yelled. "Those weren't fireworks! It was that new bomb!"

I exchanged looks with the factory supervisor. His eyes weren't smiling any more.

"Someone's dropped the bomb? But who?"

"How should I know?"

"Should we call the ministry?"

I shook my head – I didn't care one way or the other. We were done for anyway. I just wanted to spend the rest of my time quietly; I didn't care what might or might not happen, and in any case, many more people would die if the army were mobilized. I tried to console myself with that thought.

"You should go home," I said. The factory supervisor had only recently married.

"What about you then?" he asked.

"It doesn't matter. I live too far away. I don't think I'd last that long."

"But . . ." He stared at me as if he wanted to say something. Then he looked down. After a few moments, he lifted his face, looked at me again and stretched out a hand.

"Right. See you then."

We shook hands at the western end of the square.

I watched as he strode off along my lengthening shadow and crossed the square toward the underground concourse. A rainbow appeared in the spray of fountain water as it glinted in the sunlight. The factory supervisor stopped beside the fountain and turned to look back at me. I nodded, then he disappeared into the distance beyond the fountain spray.

I started to walk along the terrace. I felt terribly sleepy.

I would never see the night again. It would be followed by a milk-white morning with pink eyes, as usual, but there would be no taste of toothpaste that morning; there would be no smell of coffee. It would just be a morning. No one would be there to see it; no one would wake up, and no one would come to sprinkle water on the square. I wondered what my wife was doing. Was she already asleep?

I should have been prepared for this – I'd known about it for a long time. Once the war started, this part of town was bound to be attacked first, as it was where all the munitions factories were.

A cool breeze blew again.

A girl of seven or eight was standing in front of a drinks vending machine next to a huge potted palm. She was sucking her thumb and swaying her head slowly from side to side. When I approached her, she looked up at me with her thumb still in her mouth. She wore a blue dress with white polka dots and had her hair tied back. I thought my wife might have looked like that when she was a child.

"What's the matter?" I asked. "Do you want a drink?"

The girl nodded. "I'm thirsty," she said in a thin little voice.

I put two coins in the vending machine. A paper cup dropped down, and the machine filled it with bright green juice. The girl's pale throat made little movements as she gulped the juice down. Then she breathed out and leaned forward against the vending machine, as if she felt safe now. The surface of the machine was so cold that little beads of water clung to it. She pressed her white forehead against the red metal of the machine and started giggling to herself; she seemed to find her sleepiness funny. Her forehead was perspiring slightly. Eventually, she began to slide slowly down to the ground. I picked up her limp body, took her onto the terrace and laid her on a vacant deck chair there. She was already cold.

There was hardly anyone about now. A few people were walking slowly across the square; many others were slumped over the tables where they sat. They were probably dead already.

The sun still beat down relentlessly.

I went back into the beer hall and called home from a telephone beside the counter. There was no answer.

I walked through the beer hall into the garden at the back. Outside, I passed some tropical palms and saw a wooden house painted white. The door was open, so I walked in. An old man with white whiskers and a healthy color to his face was sitting at a table in the middle of the room. He was drinking beer. The windows were all open, but the cooler was still on.

The old man had a look in his eye as if he knew everything there was to know. "Is it hot outside?" he asked, smiling at me genially.

"Yes. But it's nice and cool in here."

"I suggest you stay here, then."

"Well, if I'm not disturbing you . . ."

"Will you have a beer?"

"No, thanks."

There was a double bed in a corner of the room.

"My wife is with her folks in the country right now," said the old man.

"Do you own the beer hall?"

"Yes. Sure you won't have a beer?"

"No, really. Thanks."

"So how about having a lie-down? You look awfully sleepy."

The old man pointed to the bed.

"Don't you mind?"

"Of course not. You sleep on the side nearest the wall. I'll join you soon."

"All right."

119

I was so sleepy that I could hardly keep my eyes open. I went toward the bed, took off my shoes and placed them neatly beside it. The old man was still drinking his beer and looking out of the window.

"I wonder how many will die? I really would like to know," he muttered.

I lay down on the bed, loosened my tie and unfastened the top button of my shirt.

"I wonder how many will die," the old man said again. He got up and came over to me. "Aren't you hot?" he asked.

"Not really," I replied.

"I could close the windows. Then the cooler will work better."

"No, no. This is just fine."

The old man took off his shirt and lay on the bed next to me.

"The bed is more comfortable if you lie on your side," he said.

I turned to face the wall. Yes, it was more comfortable that way. The old man turned to face the other side.

"I wonder how many will die," he muttered once more. "Goodnight, then."

"Goodnight."

The old man started to snore immediately, but quietly and with a healthy rhythm.

I closed my eyes.

As my mind started to dim, I thought about my wife. After a while, I thought about my dead mother. Then I thought about my wife again.

And then I fell asleep.

Cross Section

THE PROFESSOR HAD INVITED a group of reporters to a presentation in his living room. "An ongoing problem in historical geology," he started, "is how to research geological strata. Until now, there have been only two ways of investigating strata *in situ*. One is to actually go and inspect locations where sections have been exposed by the forces of nature; the other involves using heavy machinery to excavate land where we think interesting strata might be present. Needless to say, both of these methods are extremely costly in terms of time, money and effort."

* * *

The professor's wife was frustrated.

Her husband immersed himself night and day in his research on historical geology and didn't give a moment's thought to her physical needs.

It was driving her mad; no one had any idea how frustrated she was. She had inherited a fortune from her father, a multi-millionaire, and to the outside world seemed to lack nothing. Besides, she was beautiful. No one ever imagined for a single moment that the professor – however enslaved he might be to his weighty studies – would leave such a beautiful woman to her own devices night after night.

* * *

"This problem has hampered research on geological strata and greatly obstructed the progress of historical geology. So I have been trying to devise a simple method that will enable us to observe geological strata with absolute clarity, however tricky the location. I have conducted research in fields outside my special area, such as mechanical engineering, electrical engineering and electronics, purely with the aim of solving this problem. And now, I have invited you all here today because, after many years of painstaking research, I have at last reached the stage where I can solve this problem. . . ."

* * *

Eventually, the professor's wife found herself a lover. She easily managed to hoodwink her husband and immersed herself in a whirl of carnal passion, both night and day. But it didn't last long; she had been sheltered as a child and knew nothing of the world, yet even she could see that her lover was only interested in her money.

"Darling, won't you divorce the professor and marry me?" her false paramour whispered in her ear one afternoon as he stroked her long black hair.

"I can't," she replied.

"You mean you still love him?" he retorted indignantly. "You've just been using me all along! All right then, I'm going to tell your husband about us. The whole thing."

So she poisoned her lover.

* * *

"When we shine a light on certain minerals, they emit a unique glow. We call this fluorescence. Actually, there are quite a lot of minerals that have this property. The origin and color of this fluorescence varies from mineral to mineral; no two minerals emit the same glow. Scheelite, for example, glows a bluish-white when exposed to ultraviolet rays. In calcite, the ions of transition elements glow, and so on. What I have done is to capture these effects and reproduce them. By combining 234 different types of light, I have invented a powerful fluoroscopic ray that can reveal the internal composition of geophysical objects."

* * *

The professor's wife was still frustrated.

It was driving her crazy. So she took a number of lovers, one after the other. Though initially attracted by her beauty, they would eventually turn their attention to her massive wealth; it was inevitable. And when they thought the time was right, they would ask her to divorce the professor. When she refused, they would threaten her, and when they threatened her, she would poison them. It turned into quite a regular thing.

* * *

"Now, if I shine my fluoroscopic ray onto the ground from above, the geological strata beneath that point will be projected onto a screen in cross-section. The returning glow from each geophysical object below the ground will be registered as a spatial coordinate, and the computer will do the rest. To demonstrate this to you today, I have erected the fluoroscopic device in my garden. There – you can see it outside the window. It is positioned such that it will cast the fluoroscopic ray down into an old dry well with nothing but earth inside. What you will see on the screen behind you is a cross-section of geological strata beneath the well. All I have to do is flip this switch."

* * *

To hide the bodies of her poisoned lovers from her husband, the professor's wife threw them into the old dry well in their garden. Each time she threw one down, she covered the corpse with soil, and the well gradually filled up as a result. When the well was completely full of corpses and soil, even the professor's wife couldn't remember how many lovers she'd poisoned and thrown down there.

* * *

The professor flipped the switch to activate his fluoroscopic device, and the reporters turned to look at the giant screen, which covered a whole wall of the room. In no time at all, the cross-section of strata in the old waterless well appeared in glorious color on the screen before them.

Narcissism

The Three Laws of Robotics according to Isaac Asimov:

First Law	A robot may not injure a human being or, through inaction, allow a human being to come to harm.
Second Law	A robot must obey orders given it by human beings except where such orders would conflict with the First Law.
Third Law	A robot must protect its own existence as long as such protection does not conflict with the First or Second Laws.

My secondhand robot had finally arrived.

"We had quite a job finding this one, sir," the salesman said with due courtesy as he carried the coffin-shaped box into my living room. "I mean a secondhand one that matched your order precisely. In fact, we've gone to considerable pains to meet your requirements. Would you like to see it first?"

I nodded, and the salesman started prizing open the lid.

"I won't pay for it if it's not what I ordered," I said sullenly. I was in a pretty foul mood, to be honest; it was Sunday, my day off, and I didn't take kindly to being woken so early.

"One look at this robot and all your troubles will instantly disappear," the salesman said with absolute confidence as he removed the lid. "There you are, sir."

I peered into the box, and all my troubles instantly disappeared. The robot was utterly incredible.

She had a really cute face. Her eyes were a bit close together, but that was to my liking. She even had a few freckles under her eyes, and her shapely salmon-pink lips made my heart ring like a bell.

Under her dowdy maid's costume, it was easy to see how fit she was. Her breasts weren't that big, but that meant her body would be firm and taut. Her legs were perfectly proportioned, beautifully curved and narrowing at the knee and ankle.

"Fff," I snorted.

I was determined not to show any weakness. The salesman had been trying to read my expression from the moment he'd stepped in. If I'd broken into a smile, he might have tried to bump the price up. Luckily, I'm quite good at hiding my feelings, so I managed to conceal the joy that was welling up inside me – but even then, I couldn't stop my cheeks twitching once or twice.

"It's quite well made – for a robot," I said as gruffly as I could.

"Please, this is not a robot!" said the salesman, looking slightly hurt. "We like to call them 'androids' or 'humanoids', sir."

I could see his point. A robot was just a mechanical version of a human being, but an android – a humanoid – actually resembled a human in every way.

"Robot is good enough for me," I said, glaring at him. "Don't give me that jargon. It's a machine. However well designed it is, a machine is a machine. I won't bow to a machine. 'Robot' will do."

The salesman gave me a dubious look then shrugged his shoulders. "As you say, sir. Well now, let me explain something about her – I mean *it*. This little cutie's body has been made identical to the real female body in a number of ways. Under her skin is a kind of plastic that has the same elasticity as muscle. It protects the internal organs, er, machinery. I'd particularly like to mention her skin; it's more absorbent and cooler than a real woman's skin but also has a propensity to warm up under friction. Each hair has been individually implanted—"

"Enough!" I said to interrupt his patter. I was exploding with desire to get this robot naked as soon as I possibly could. "I know all about that, more or less. Just answer a couple of questions, will you?"

"Certainly, sir."

"Could it ever malfunction?"

"This little cutie is programmed to repair any malfunction by herself. She can even replace her own body parts if necessary. But there's just one part she can't repair – the electronic brain inside her head. If that were to malfunction, it would be the equivalent of a human going mad."

"Going mad? That's a bit worrying."

"Ah, but have no fear. You know the Third Law of Robotics, I presume? Even if a robot were to go mad, it could never harm a human being, for if things ever got to that point, it would self-destruct."

"But what should I do if this one does go mad?"

"Call me, and I will come and repair her myself." The salesman bowed politely.

"What about the last owner?" I said, giving him a hard look. "Why didn't he need the robot any more?"

"He passed away," the salesman answered most regretfully. "He was an unmarried company employee, like you."

"So, this robot will work as a maid and also . . ." I hesitated. "Well, I mean . . . I assume she also . . . you know . . . accompanies her owner at night . . . Yes? Yes. But I wonder if a certain *part* of her could have been, how shall I put it, *damaged* by the previous owner, if you follow my drift? Or worn out perhaps?"

"Have no fear," he answered with a smile. "As I said just now, if that had been the case, she would have repaired herself automatically, thereby keeping herself in perfect physical condition at all times. She's as good as new, you may be sure of that."

"Good." I was satisfied. "Next, I would like to hear the robot's voice."

"Certainly, sir." He leaned over the box and peered down at

the robot. "Mari-chan? It's time to greet your new master."

The robot had been lying still in the box all the while, her eyes fixed on the ceiling, but now she suddenly turned to me and winked.

I was taken aback. Where had she learned to do that?!

The robot stepped out of her box and stood in front of me, bowing deeply. "Pleased to make your acquaintance, sir. My name is Mari." She had quite a husky voice. Hmm.

I was champing at the bit now, but there was still some business to do; I couldn't afford to show any sign of weakness. "Mari? That's a human name," I said in a deliberately cantankerous tone. "A robot's a robot. From now on, your name is Robot." I turned to the salesman. "So, how much?"

The salesman quoted a price far lower than I'd expected. Even then, I insisted on a ten-percent discount. He gave this and that reason why he couldn't go any lower, but in the end he knocked ten percent off the price.

And so I had bought my robot.

* * *

As soon as the salesman had left, I started to undress the robot. I needed to inspect my goods, after all.

"Don't!" she protested with reddened cheeks, stubbornly holding down the hem of her skirt.

That didn't seem very robot-like. Still, I did my best to convince myself. *It's just a machine. I can do what I like. Ignore it.*

I ignored the robot and went to lift up her skirt. "I need to inspect my goods. Just be quiet."

"But, sir," she said, twisting her body coquettishly, "it's too early."

"Quiet! Do you mean to disobey your master?" I snapped. I thought I might rip her clothes off there and then, but then I realized that, yes, it was still quite early. I had plenty of time; there was no need to hurry. "Well, all right. Go and make some coffee then."

"Certainly." She gave a little bow, did a crisp about-turn and headed for the kitchen.

I gazed at her pleasantly slender waist and swinging hips as she left the room, then sat on the sofa and waited for my coffee. I was alone, so I could allow a broad smile to spread over my face. Now I understood why so many men were reluctant to marry these days.

When sex robots and housekeeper robots for single men first appeared on the market, not only were they technically flawed but the prices were astronomical. Yet even then, men who'd had enough of relationships with real women were falling over each other to buy them.

As the robots progressively improved, they came to rival real women in a number of ways and grew in popularity as a result. Even married men started to buy the mistress robot, the prototype robot, the No. 2, 3 and 4 robots, and so on. Soon a robot that combined the functions of sex and housekeeping services appeared. Outraged women formed lobby groups and launched an opposition movement. A Sex Robot Prohibition Bill was debated in parliament. But around that time, leading academics who supported the robots issued a joint declaration stating that "sex robots are healthier than masturbating."

The bill was rejected.

Oddly, a male sex robot for women was never developed. That did kind of make sense, though, as the manufacturers were all men; the sexual needs of women were the last thing on their minds. Instead, they just kept bringing out different female robots.

First, robots with different personalities, different skin colors and different physical attributes became widely available, as did male robots without male attributes – in other words, homosexual robots (known as homobots). These were followed by masobots, sadobots, Lolibots and grannibots for perverts; duobots for twin freaks; nowaybots with sealed vaginas – I couldn't quite see what *they* were for – and even buttbots for fans of the female rear.

It was then that words like "android" and "humanoid" came to replace "robot" in everyday usage.

I was still a low-level worker and could hardly afford to buy one of these devices, though I'd heard a lot about them. So for a while, I merely observed this new consumer frenzy from the sidelines. Of course, I could have bought a masturbatory android for students or a buttoid, nothing but a pair of buttocks, as those were relatively cheap. But I didn't, because I really wasn't that bothered – and anyway, thanks to the sex robot boom, the streets were crawling with jilted women on the lookout for a man. That meant I could have a one-night stand with no strings attached any time I wanted. For women, on the other hand, finding a marriage partner had never been so hard.

As time went on, I got promoted and needed to worry less about money. I moved into a big new apartment, and that was when I started to think of buying a robot. I'd discovered that, if you knew where to look, you could find secondhand robots that were as good as new but considerably cheaper.

Then again, I never expected to find anything as good as this one; I was over the moon. My whole body tingled with anticipation when I imagined what it would be like to take her to bed that night and enjoy her.

She came in with the coffee and passed it to me with perfectly feminine grace. I felt a warm sensation inside; I was so starved of home comforts as it was. My heart began to soften. But that wouldn't do at all. I immediately snapped out of it. What was I getting so sentimental about? She was just a machine! Just a sex doll.

"How is it?" she asked, tilting her head cutely.

I took a sip. "Not bad," I answered with a nod. "But next time make it hotter."

"OK," she said, bowing slightly. "Shall I clean the apartment now?"

"Oh, yes, of course."

I wanted to talk to her some more, but caught myself in time. Wanting to talk to a machine? Ridiculous! What was I turning into?

I continued to treat her with indifference for the rest of the day but still watched her surreptitiously as she busied herself with the cleaning, cooking and washing. I so desperately wanted to touch her body, take her in my arms, but I didn't want to be rejected again, so I held back. Being cold-shouldered by a machine twice in one day would have been quite beneath my dignity.

Her movements, her expressions, her way of talking – they all had an air of elegant refinement that was quite lacking in contemporary women. Well, of course they did. The men who created her had given her everything men wanted but contemporary women lacked.

I could think of nothing but making love to her. I tried to read, I tried to watch TV, but my mind was definitely elsewhere. My anticipation of our bed play was about to reach bursting point when at last dusk fell. I couldn't wait a second longer, so I flew into the kitchen, where she was still clearing up the dinner things.

"Right. Come on. It's time now!" I commanded, grabbing her firmly by the arm.

She opened her beautifully limpid eyes wide and stared at me in surprise, then lowered her long lashes coyly.

"Time?" she said. "Time for what?"

"Don't play innocent!" I was getting quite irritated now; my voice was louder than I would have liked. "Do I have to explain everything? Right. Now you'll be your master's bed partner. You understand? Bloody machine!" And I pulled her toward the bedroom.

"Ow! You're hurting me!" she moaned tearfully. "Please be gentler!"

"Shut up!" I yelled as I stripped off. "Why should I follow that rigmarole with a machine? Please be gentler? Ha. You sound like a real woman. I've paid good money precisely to avoid all that bother! You understand? Now just take your clothes off!"

"Oh! Please don't talk like that!" The android covered her face with both hands and started to cry. Her previous owner must have really spoiled her.

I decided I would have to teach her a lesson. As she made no attempt to undress, I went up to her, grabbed the white collar of her navy blue maid's outfit with both hands and ripped the bodice open.

"Don't!" she gasped. In her surprise, she put her hands to her chest and tried to hide her white bra. "You don't have to be so mean!"

"Mean? What's that got to do with it? I own you, for God's sake!" I grabbed her skirt and ripped that off too. "I can do what I like with my own property! Understand? Anything I like!"

She started to cry uncontrollably, but I ignored her and pulled off her underwear. "After all, those tears are just salt water. Quite convincing, though."

Disregarding her floods of tears, I pushed her down onto the bed and frantically forced myself into her firm yet yielding body.

* * *

Was it sex or masturbation? Whatever the case, I was finished in no time. Maybe it was because the frustration had been building up for so long. My expectations had been too high, and I was frankly disappointed. For, contrary to the company's promises, my robot didn't respond even slightly; it just kept whimpering beneath me.

There again, it was just a machine, wasn't it? Whether or not it responded was none of my concern.

I made love to my robot several more times in succession, partly out of frustration. After a while I started to feel drowsy, then fell into a deep, deep sleep.

The next morning, I awoke with a huge sneeze. The room felt awfully cold. I turned to see the robot's naked body snuggled up next to me under the duvet.

"Hey!" I shouted. "What's this? Robots aren't supposed to sleep with humans!"

Her eyes opened instantly. "I'm not sleeping," she said with a smile. "I'm just lying here."

I looked at my watch and was shocked to see the time: it was nearly eight o'clock. "Shit! I'll be late for work!" Now I was really getting mad.

"Haven't you made the breakfast yet? Not even the coffee?"

She ignored my rebuke and started to stroke my chest. "Do you remember last night?" she said with complete calm. "You were so *wild*!"

"Never mind about that. Get up quick and make breakfast. Get my clothes ready."

She started rubbing my cheek with her forehead. "Did you want me that badly? How was I then? Was I good?"

"It's none of your business!" I raged. "And why's it so cold in here?"

"It's your fault," she replied with a wink. "You forced me into bed while I was still tidying up, so the fridge was left open all night."

"What? Go and close it then. Go on!" I tried to push her out of the bed. "Quick! You'll make me late for work!"

"My previous master wasn't this rough!" she said reproachfully. "He was much gentler."

I glared at her. "Listen. If you say that again, you'll wish you hadn't. I'm your master now, and don't you forget it. Right, now up you get, quick!"

"Don't you think I'm cute?" she asked with a hurt look.

"What you do mean 'cute'? You're just a machine!"

The robot burst into tears.

"All right. All right! You're cute, OK? You're cute!"

She hunched her shoulders and pouted. "Say it as if you mean it! Go on, say I'm beautiful! Say I was fantastic last night!"

"OK. You were fantastic last night." I suppressed my anger and tried to caress her as gently as I could. "You're beautiful."

"You wanted me so badly last night you couldn't wait any longer, right?"

"Right. I couldn't wait."

"Mari."

"I couldn't wait, *Mari*."

"That's why you were so rough. That's why you ripped my clothes off, because you couldn't contain yourself any longer. Am I right?"

"Yes, Mari. You are right."

"So does that mean you love me?"

"Yes, Mari. It means I love you."

"Ah! Ah! Say it again."

"I love you. Mari."

"And again."

"That's enough!" I yelled. "You're getting worse than a real woman! Cut it out right now, or I'll smack you one!" She burst into tears again and ran into the bathroom, naked.

This was no time to be dawdling. After several loud sneezes, I reluctantly got up, took my clothes out of the drawer and went to the kitchen to close the fridge door. Mari still hadn't emerged from the bathroom.

"I'm on my way now," I shouted. "By the time I get back I want to see all the cleaning and laundry done and dinner on the table. Got it?" And with that I hurried out of the apartment.

Later that day, I phoned the robot salesman from work.

"What do you mean by selling me such a narcissistic robot?" I bawled at him. "I've caught a cold thanks to her! What are you going to do about it?"

I told the salesman the whole story.

"That's funny. Quite unusual," he said. "She was perfectly normal when I inspected her."

"The previous owner must have indulged her too much. He must have pampered her, praised her too much, and that's why she's such a narcissist. It must be!"

"I beg to differ," said the salesman. "It's meeting you that's made her that way. You've treated her too roughly, I think. I've seen this before: your rough treatment has knocked her confidence, and she's trying to regain it by being narcissistic. You see, in psychological terms, narcissism is a kind of reaction—"

"No. It's definitely because she's been spoiled," I argued. "Anyway, I can't have her like this. Come and repair her immediately."

"All right. I'll be there this evening."

Evening was already setting in by the time I returned to the apartment. It was getting dark outside, but none of the lights were on.

"Hey! Where are you?" I called.

I switched on the lights and looked around. The apartment was exactly as I'd left it that morning, with no sign that any cleaning had been done at all. When I went to the kitchen, I found the things from the previous night still lying where they'd been left.

"Where are you?" I shouted. Anger rose in the pit of my stomach as I opened the bathroom door.

And there she was, stark naked. I stood in the doorway, barely comprehending what I saw. The robot was standing in front of the full-length mirror and masturbating with her eyes half-closed, giving out little gasps all the while. Oil dribbled from the corner of her mouth – a substitute for saliva. I'd called her a machine, and her confidence had been knocked, so she was trying to regain it by comforting herself.

"Have you been doing that since this morning, when you should have been doing your work?" I bellowed. "You stupid, useless machine!"

"Stop it!" she pleaded, turning to me with disheveled hair. "Don't call me names!"

"Why not? That's what you are, isn't it? You're just a machine! An ugly machine made to look human! Just looking at you makes me want to vomit!"

"Please stop it," she said and, without warning, placed her hand over my mouth.

She had extraordinary strength, the strength of a machine. My efforts to remove her hand were in vain; it was clamped so hard over my mouth that my cheeks began to ache. All I could do was flail wildly with my arms and legs.

"Forgive me," she said, still blocking my mouth with her hand. "If you insult me any more, I will break down. I must protect myself. But don't worry, I won't do you any harm. After all, you can breathe through your nose if your mouth is closed, right?"

But I'd caught a cold that morning. My nose was blocked.

Sadism

— 1 —

Ishida called from reception. He sounded pretty agitated.

"You know that TV celebrity Hisako Toba?" he said. "She's here right now. And she's hopping mad."

"Yeah? What about?"

"You know what about! That sex doll we made! She wants to know who's responsible for it!"

"That'd be me."

"Right. So what do you want me to do?"

"Leave it to me," I sighed. "I'm on my way."

Hisako Toba was sitting impatiently in the reception lounge when I arrived. Sitting next to her was a man who I guessed was her lawyer.

No sooner had I introduced myself than she set upon me. "You've made a sex doll that resembles me!" she shrieked. She looked as mad as hell. "It's got my face, my voice, even my personality!"

"I'm afraid that's just not possible," I said with a forced smile and a patronizing shake of the head. "Whenever we make a doll in someone's likeness, we always get the person's consent first. And we pay a lot of money for it, I might add. We simply couldn't make a doll that looks like you without your permission."

"Unbelievable," she hissed, rolling her eyes sarcastically. "There are women who actually give their consent? I would never agree to such a thing however much you paid me!"

"Really?" I said, smiling affably and shaking my head again. "Well, luckily for us, there are plenty of women who are only too happy to give their consent; actually, we almost have to beat them off these days. They actually offer *us* money to make sex dolls of them. Why? I'll tell you. It's because *not* having a doll made of them means they're not fancied. And being celebrities, they have to keep up their image, their popularity, or they'll fall by the wayside. That includes being fancied. In fact, there's at least one famous actress whose popularity nosedived because she didn't have a doll made quickly enough."

"I never heard anything so insulting in all my life!" Toba arched her eyebrows even higher than they were already. "Any woman who has a sex doll made of her will ruin her own reputation. And, anyway, look at *me*! I haven't had one made, yet I'm as popular as ever. So you've pirated my image, and that proves my point. You wouldn't have done that if I weren't popular, would you?"

"We haven't pirated anything," I replied indignantly. "We haven't made a doll that resembles you in any way, so there's nothing we could have pirated. Anyway, where have you seen this doll you're talking about?"

"I haven't seen it!" she snapped, pursing her lips in frustration. "What do you take me for? I know about it because it's all over the gossip magazines. But he's seen it," she said, pointing at the man I'd guessed was her lawyer. "And he's my lawyer."

The man took a photograph out of his breast pocket. "This is it," he said. "One of your products, for sure – a sex doll that resembles Ms Toba in almost every way. You have made this doll without Ms Toba's consent, thereby infringing on her human rights, illegally using her image rights, and moreover violating both the Sex Doll Act and the Act to Promote the Proper Manufacture and Use of Androids."

"Hmm," I mused as I eyed the photograph. "It's a bit out of focus. Taken by some kid, no doubt."

"I took it," the lawyer said stony-faced.

"Oh, I'm so sorry," I said, making a slight bow in mock apology. I looked at the picture again. "I can't say for sure from this photo, but if it is one of ours, it would have to be in the R5 range."

"Correct," affirmed the lawyer, whipping out a notebook. "The model number is R5-13M 1095."

"You mean you actually wrote down the number? If only you'd said that earlier!" I turned to Ishida, who was standing next to me. "Fetch an R5-13M 1095 from the warehouse and bring it here, will you?"

Ishida's mouth was agape with astonishment. "What, here?"

"Yes, here," I replied, controlling my irritation.

"Are you sure?" he said. He looked quite worried now.

"Yes, I'm sure. Fetch one please. Quickly!"

Ishida's knees were knocking as he walked out of the reception lounge.

I gave Hisako Toba another weary smile. "As you know, our sex dolls are made with very great precision; they're not so much sex dolls as androids. The ones we used to make, up until about ten years ago, were little more than machines. Robots. But thanks to subsequent advances in robotics, we started to produce robots that were identical to humans. They were light years away from the old concept of robots, and that's why we called them androids. It means 'human-like.' And after—"

"I know all that," Toba cut in irritably. "Spare me your lecture."

"But there's more!" I continued nonetheless. "After a while, things had progressed so far that most men were thinking the same thing: *I wonder if I could have sex with one.*"

"Disgusting!" Toba retorted with venom. "Only a man with a filthy mind would think that!"

"Really? Don't you think there's a good reason why these androids are so popular now? There is! It's because women have become too domineering and men are sick of it! If they get married they're worked like dogs, and if they want a divorce they're sued for every penny!"

"That's because men have lost their self-respect."

"Maybe. But there are still some who want to work hard,

even at the expense of having a family. They don't want to be saddled with mortgages and school fees, so they stay single and concentrate on their work. But the problem is how these men should relieve their sexual needs. We don't have red-light districts any more, so they get frustrated and can't focus on their work. That's why the government passed the Sex Doll Act."

The lawyer piped up again. "Ah, yes, the Sex Doll Act. I believe you'll find a clause in it expressly prohibiting the manufacture and sale of a sex doll that clearly resembles a specific person without first obtaining that person's consent."

"Indeed. But you know, men will always idolize beautiful women, especially if they're well known. By making love to a beautiful woman who's popular among his peers, a man can satisfy his desire for conquest, his thirst for power and his need to dominate, all in one go. If you want proof, look at the sales of sex dolls made to resemble famous TV personalities."

"I suppose you always get their consent?"

"Of course."

"So what are you going to do if this sex doll looks like me?" asked Hisako Toba. Just then, in walked Ishida with the R5-13M 1095.

– 2 –

"Well, here it is," I said. "Have a good look. Tell me if it resembles Ms Toba."

It resembled Ms Toba. I was trying to sound confident, but I was quaking inside. In fact, the android didn't just resemble Hisako Toba; it was exactly the same in every conceivable way – height, proportions, face, expression, voice, even personality.

Ishida was quaking too. But I had a plan.

"So, how about it?" I asked the lawyer. "Is this the one you saw?"

"It's the one!" the lawyer replied, red-faced with anger. "And you're seriously saying this doll doesn't resemble Ms Toba? You must be bloody joking. They're exactly the same! Who are you trying to kid?"

"Wait a minute," Toba interrupted. She got up, walked over

to the android and looked at it closely. "Does it really look that much like me?"

"What are you saying?" the lawyer gasped in disbelief. "It resembles you in every way!"

"My nose isn't that big, for a start. And the eyes are too narrow."

"There you are," I declared triumphantly. "They aren't alike!"

"What are you gawking at?" snapped the android, glaring at Hisako Toba. "Patronizing bitch!"

Toba seemed startled at first – not at the android's language, but at how closely its voice resembled hers. But she soon regained her composure and snapped back. "Who the hell do you think you are? You're just a damned robot!"

"I am not a robot!" the android screamed with a mad look in its eyes.

"Oh, dear. It's getting hysterical," Toba said with infuriating calm as she turned to her lawyer. "I never get hysterical. My voice isn't that gravelly. I've got more class than that."

"Class? Don't make me laugh!" yelled the android.

"But surely you must agree," the lawyer said in desperation, ignoring the android's outburst. "You must agree there is a resemblance."

"You know, I find that quite insulting?" Toba said with a frown.

Much as I was enjoying their altercation, we couldn't allow our product to insult visiting celebrities indefinitely; it wasn't good for business. "Android," I ordered, "come and sit over here."

The android came and slumped down rudely next to me. Its skirt rode up as it sat, completely exposing its thighs.

Hisako Toba went back to her own seat, doing her best to look refined. "I'm not that undignified. I've got better manners than that — that — *thing*."

"Absolutely. Absolutely," I agreed, nodding several times. "It's not like you at all."

"Oh, for heaven's sake! They are identical!" protested the lawyer. His voice was starting to rise as he grew more frantic.

"We are not identical!" the android wailed with its mouth opened wide. "I think I would die if I resembled her!"

Hisako Toba opened her mouth wide and yelled at her lawyer. "Would I open my mouth wide and yell like that? No, I wouldn't! You have got to be joking!"

"I'm not saying that!" the lawyer blathered as he wiped the sweat from his brow. "But if you're not alike, why have I come all the way here to prove it? What the hell am I doing here anyway?" He puffed out his chest in a show of pride. "I am a qualified professional, I'll have you know. And in my professional judgement, that sex doll is an exact likeness of you. You're identical!" he exclaimed loudly.

"I am not a sex doll!" screamed the sex doll.

Toba suddenly stood up and turned on the lawyer. "You're trying to insult me, aren't you?" she said. "I'm not having this!"

"Why do you have to be so damn stubborn?" yelled the lawyer, almost on the verge of tears.

"You're fired!" shouted Toba.

"You're the worst client I ever had!" the lawyer shouted back.

The android leapt to its feet and punched the air. "Go, lawyer man! Give it to her!"

"See what I mean?" bawled the lawyer. "Exactly the same! Even the spiteful remarks!"

"Get out of my sight!" Toba ordered, as if it were *her* office building.

"Case rejected! Go to hell!" the lawyer raged as he stormed out.

I turned to Toba with another duplicitous smile. "Heh, what's got into him?" I said disingenuously. "There's no resemblance at all, is there."

"No. There is no resemblance!" she replied angrily.

My plan had worked perfectly.

Humans hate anyone who resembles them. It's a kind of fear, an instinct for self-preservation, and it tends to be much more pronounced in women. A woman is never going to admit that she resembles another whose failings are the same as her own.

After all, there are precious few people who know their failings and are willing to admit them in the first place; most aren't even remotely aware of them. That was particularly true of Hisako Toba, a woman who was both headstrong and incredibly self-centered. She had often played headstrong, self-centered women in her acting career and had won numerous plaudits for it. She thought it was because she was a good actress, but, in fact, she was just playing herself all the time.

"By the way," she said after calming down a little. "I suppose you could be right. It could be good publicity for an actress to have a sex doll made of her."

"Definitely. So how about it?" I asked. "Can we make one of you?"

"It would have be refined, intelligent, and well-mannered. Are you sure you could manage that?"

"Of course," I replied, rubbing my hands together. "We can easily make a doll that's refined, intelligent and well-mannered. Just like you."

"Huh! That's a laugh," snarled the android. I gave it a murderous stare.

"All right. I'll be back," said Toba.

"Perfect. Bye for now."

And with that, Hisako Toba walked out of the reception lounge.

"Phew, that was close," said Ishida, wiping the sweat from his face. "Amazing, isn't it? They're completely identical, yet she refused to admit it."

"Well, that's women for you," I said with a pained laugh.

"But don't you think it's strange?" Ishida continued. "We make a sex doll in the exact likeness of Hisako Toba, even down to her headstrong selfishness and her disdain for men. And yet it's so popular with men that it's flying off the shelves! What do you think they see in her?"

"We did some research on that. Men have an aggressive instinct, a destructive urge. If it's harnessed properly, it can help them in their work, but sometimes they want to direct it at women. The trouble is women today are looking for kind, considerate men;

they tend to dislike the rough ones. That provides the perfect environment for women like Hisako Toba to thrive. So then we thought if we made dolls that resembled women like her, men could satisfy those urges without hurting anyone. They're just androids, you see; they don't have feelings, so it doesn't matter if they get treated roughly or knocked about. It's a kind of catharsis for men, a kind of channel for mental healing."

"I see! By treating a headstrong, self-centered woman roughly, we satisfy our primeval need to dominate."

"Exactly. Our primeval instinct, survival of the species and all that."

"I wouldn't mind having one myself." Ishida's eyes glistened as he ogled the R5 android made in the likeness of Hisako Toba.

"Not if I can help it!" sneered the android, glaring back at him with open hostility.

– 3 –

I stayed on to do some overtime. There was still a lot of paperwork to deal with, and, besides, the incident with Hisako Toba had put me back a bit. After I'd signed everything off, I sat at my desk and lit a cigarette to help me relax. I didn't need to hurry home, as I wasn't married; I was far too busy for that.

I had dozens of sex dolls at home, all made by my company. "Taking work home", I liked to call it. But I'd never used the R5 type, the one that resembled Hisako Toba.

I'll try it out tonight, I thought. The R5 from the warehouse would still be sitting in the reception lounge; I would take it home and fill out the paperwork the next day. That was one of our favorite perks as employees – we got a fifty percent discount on goods in stock.

I went back to the reception lounge and found the R5 still slouched on the sofa.

"About time!" The android sat up and immediately started bristling for a fight. I marveled at the precision and skill of our engineers. It was as if Hisako Toba herself were in the room.

"Shut it!" I barked to halt her tirade. "You're coming home with me. Let's go."

She said nothing but looked me up and down for a few moments. Eventually, she sniggered derisively and turned away.

Flipping androids! I was starting to get mad now.

"Come on! Chop chop!" I said, grabbing her firmly by the arm.

"Take your hands off me!" she yelled as she pulled her arm free.

She was remarkably strong, even for an android. I was momentarily stunned.

"Huh!" she sneered, observing me through a corner of her eye. Her mouth was distorted in an icy smile that was patently full of malice.

That was when I finally lost it. "Damned robot!" I screamed as I lunged at her. I felt like ravishing her there and then.

"I am not a robot!" she said, pushing me back. "All right?"

A half-crazy, sadistic impulse started to well up inside me; I hadn't felt so excited for ages. It was incredibly arousing.

"Robot!" I yelled, slapping her hard on the cheek. She gasped in shock and rolled her eyes.

Before she could recover, I grabbed her jacket and pulled it off.

"You're crazy!" she screamed, opening her red mouth wide. "Who do you think you are?"

A tingling sensation of pleasure raced down my spine. Yes, I was starting to see why this one sold so well. If I'd done that to a real woman, I'd have been had up for assault, at the very least. But it was all right; it was just a robot. And unlike other sex robots, the R5-type had been designed to resist until the bitter end. That merely heightened the thrill.

The android ran behind the sofa in an attempt to escape.

"Oh, no, you don't!" I yelled as I vaulted over the sofa. I took hold of the android and ripped off her blouse. Now her pale pink flesh was exposed. Her cheek was red from the slap I'd given her, but that was to be expected; the skin of the R5-type was made of a special plastic that reddened when warm.

145

The android played her part well. Her artificial brain quickly seemed to realize there was no escape, so she switched to the ploy of shrieking hysterically while clawing at my face with her nails.

Excellent. I grabbed her arm firmly with one hand and pulled off her skirt with the other, completely exposing her realistic pink thighs and black knickers.

"You're an animal! You're not human!" she screamed. And the more she screamed, the more my excitement grew. Her nails had scratched my face, and it was starting to bleed. Well, there was realism and there was realism, but never mind – it was all part of the chase. I ripped off her bra as roughly as I could and pushed her down on the sofa. Of course, she continued to resist; she was designed to. She opened her mouth and tried to bite me. She tried to kick me. She even tried to wring my neck. It was starting to resemble a good old wrestling match.

I received a vicious kick full in the abdomen, and the sudden pain made me double over and cry out in agony. The robot had incredible strength, but, of course, the pre-designed effect was to stimulate the man's desire and magnify his lust for aggression. I could see that, and the pain started to feel more like pleasure.

I punched her hard in the face. Something that looked like blood immediately started flowing from the edge of her lip. Of course, that was because her mouth was padded with rubber pouches full of red dye. Her expression of pain was terribly realistic, almost too convincing for an android; I made a mental note to congratulate the engineers. I grew more excited still and pulled her black knickers down.

Now she was grinding her teeth in anger. It was a fantastic expression. But I ignored it and planted myself inside her body as she continued to lash out at me.

As the action progressed, she kept screaming in what sounded like pain mixed with ecstasy. She panted as she arched her back and went into spasms. Suddenly, the memory of Hisako Toba's sneering attitude came back to me. She'd been sneering at men in general; that's what she'd been doing. Now I could take out all those frustrations on the R5-type android, make her suffer for all those past humiliations, not just from Toba, but from all women like her. In a fit of uncontrollable rage, I grabbed a glass ashtray from the desk next to the sofa and repeatedly brought it down hard on her head. She cried out in pain.

"Please don't! Please don't!" she'd been programmed to cry.

"Why not?" I yelled. "Now I'll give you some more!"

In the end, I put my hands around her neck and seized it in a viselike grip. I kept squeezing and squeezing for what seemed like aeons. It felt so good.

The android eventually lost consciousness, and blood trickled out of its nose. Of course, androids are nothing more than machines, however sophisticated their design. A machine obviously couldn't lose consciousness; the information that humans usually lose consciousness when strangled must have been programmed into the little electronic brain inside its head.

The R5-type was bleeding. In other words, it was a "virgin"; it had been programmed to bleed on the first occasion. Well, of course this was the first occasion – it was fresh out of the factory.

The android was now slumped lifelessly on the sofa. If it were human, it would have been dead, but being a machine, it was just out of order. Perhaps I shouldn't have treated it quite so roughly, I thought with a twinge of regret. Those androids were by no means cheap to repair.

The house phone in a corner of the reception lounge rang.

I picked up the receiver. "Yes?"

"Ah, there you are!" It was Ishida. "Where on earth have you been? I've been looking all over for you."

"Is there a problem?" I asked.

"Well, you know that Toba woman. She came back soon after that. She wants us to make a sex doll in her likeness."

"OK. Good. Where is she?"

"Erm . . . Isn't she with you?"

"No. . . ."

"I took her to reception and left her in the lounge. I said you'd be right along. Isn't she there?"

"No," I replied. "She hasn't been here. It's just me and the R5-type."

"Eh? The android? I took it back to the warehouse after that."

"Well, it must have come back."

"It couldn't have. I switched it off and removed its controls."

"So, who's slumped here on the sofa then?"

I dropped the receiver and sank weakly to the floor.

The Wind

"Listen! Someone's knocking at the door."

"No, it's just the wind."

"Really? It doesn't sound like the wind. It sounds like someone knocking."

"But the wind sometimes sounds like that."

"That's what you always say."

"Yes. And it always turns out to be the wind."

"So it does. But this time it might be someone knocking."

"Who then? Who would be knocking at this time of night?"

"True, at this time of night. Ah, there it is again. At this time of night . . . That's what bothers me."

"Even if it is someone knocking, it can't be anyone respectable. Not at this time of night."

"Well, I suppose not."

"And even if it is someone respectable, they can't be up to any good."

"Not at this time of night."

"No one comes to see us at night. No one wants to see us anyway. They only come when they need something from us."

"You know that's not true."

"All right. Sometimes they come because they have a grudge against us. There are plenty of people like that, though if you ask me they've got it all wrong. They only have a grudge against us because they can't have a grudge against themselves."

"No, no, no. I'm not talking about them."

149

Yasutaka Tsutsui

"So who are you talking about? Jiro?"

"Ah! I would be so happy if it were Jiro. Do you think he still has that beige coat?"

"He won't come back."

"Won't he? Even if he needs money?"

"Definitely not then."

"You're probably right. He was always so proud."

"Well, that's not such a bad thing, is it? After all the nasty things he said, it would take more than money to bring him back. He would have to be really desperate."

"What would you do if he came back?"

"Well, he would be down to his very last hope, but I would still send him packing. No, I won't have any more tea, thanks."

"I will."

"If I drink any more I'll be off to the bathroom all night. I hate that. It's so cold in there."

"I don't mind. At least it's indoors, and it's warm."

"Is it?"

"Ah. There it is again, that knocking sound."

"Look, if someone were there, they would knock harder, wouldn't they."

"Maybe they don't want to."

"What, out of politeness? You think Jiro has come back and is knocking politely?"

"Hmm. He's not that kind of person, is he?"

"Too right he isn't."

"Listen. There it is again."

"We'll have to change the door. We can't have it making a noise every time the wind blows."

"You've been saying that for years!"

"Yes, because you keep saying we don't need to."

"And I still say that. What, just because the wind makes a noise? We only need fit a doorbell."

"But if someone pressed it at night, we would have to go and see."

"So we could fit one of those, you know, intercom things."

150

"Then we'd have to talk to people. You should know I don't like talking to people."

"But you weren't always like that."

"No. And people took advantage. So then I started hating myself for being such an easy touch. I even started thinking it would be better to be hated than be taken for a fool. I wonder when that was."

"You really were deceived a lot, weren't you? I hated it too. I understand how you felt."

"It was horrible."

"I couldn't sleep at night."

"There's the noise again."

"Yes. And it didn't sound anything like the wind, did it?"

"But I'm sure it's the wind. No one would come and see us at this time of night, I know they wouldn't."

"What, no one at all?"

"No one."

"But it could be someone you're not expecting, someone who might surprise you."

"Who would that be, then? You can't be thinking of Ichiro, surely."

"Goodness, that was more than thirty years ago, wasn't it?"

"Yes. We had a hard time, didn't we."

"And for thirty years, it's always been the same. Whenever the wind makes a noise on the door, you say it could be Ichiro."

"Until just recently you used to go and look."

"No, I stopped going more than ten years ago."

"There's no chance of Ichiro coming back. After all, he would be thirty-eight now, if he were still alive."

"So he would. In that case, he would have come back long ago."

"I suppose so."

"So, do you think he really was kidnapped?"

"I don't know. We had that funny phone call, didn't we. But he'd already been reported missing by then, so it was probably just a prank call."

"Yes, probably. After all, they only said they were looking after him."

151

"They didn't mention a ransom or anything."

"The next two or three years were horrible, weren't they?"

"Yes. I kept dreaming about him."

"You would often wake up crying."

"Whenever someone knocked, you would rush to the door thinking it was Ichiro. Then you'd come back in tears because it wasn't him."

"Ha ha."

"Ha ha ha."

"Ah. Ichiro had such a noble face."

"I've been having happier memories of him recently."

"Me too. We couldn't even talk about him before, could we?"

"It's probably because we're getting older."

"Or because we think we'll be joining him soon."

"Yes, maybe. But we're happy anyway. We should see it like that. After all, we're not alone, are we?"

"I agree. At least we have each other."

"Other people might have larger families, but if they don't get on well and the family breaks up, they can feel so lonely. There are a lot of people like that."

"At least we have each other. We never have to feel lonely."

"That's right. Never lonely."

"Ah – it was definitely a knock that time."

"No, it was the wind."

"Are you sure? I clearly heard two knocks. Knock, knock."

"The wind."

"Yes, probably. But I might just go and look."

"Leave it, I say. It's just the wind."

"I know, but . . ."

"Does it bother you that much?"

"Yes."

"All right, go and look then. It's been a while since you went, after all."

"That's true. Ha ha."

"Ha ha ha."

"So, who was it?"

"It was the wind after all."

"But I thought I heard a man's voice."

"Yes. It was a man who called himself the wind."

"The wind?"

"That's right. I knew it as soon as I saw him. Ah, he must be the wind, I thought. You see, there was no wind blowing at all. Yet his hair was flapping. So was his white silk scarf. He was smiling. When I stared at him, he looked embarrassed and said he hadn't come for any particular reason. Well, of course. What would the wind ever want with us? But he just came anyway. He seemed a really nice person. Ah. If only he'd come earlier."

"No, I think this was the right time."

"You think so?"

"I think so. If he had come earlier, the shock would have been too great."

"That's true. He's a kind person. He knows us well. He's been thinking of us."

"Did he look like Ichiro?"

"In a way. And Jiro."

"Was he wearing a beige coat?"

"Yes. Yes! He was. A beige coat."

"So there you are. It was the wind after all."

A Vanishing Dimension

When my baby was seven months old, I bought him one of those crazy toy monkeys – the type that wears a little red hat and madly smashes cymbals together when you turn a key in its back. And that's when it all started.

Now, I'm not one of those dads who can't help showering his kids with presents. No, I bought the monkey because I've always been fascinated by them. There's something about them that intrigues me: the relentless violence of their movement, the frantic way they smash those cymbals together, that half-crazed look of eagerness on their faces.

One day, I was on my way home from the university library when I saw some in a shop window – an army of dark brown monkeys all huddled together, with a single white one in the middle. An albino toy monkey!

I couldn't resist it, so I bought the white monkey and took it home.

"A white monkey? Well, I never," said Miwa, my wife. She clearly didn't share my excitement.

At first, our son was scared of the monkey, especially when it smashed those cymbals together. But he soon got used to it, and the monkey joined the massed ranks of his little cuddly friends. Before long, in fact, it was his favorite toy; he even took it to bed with him and cried when we prized it from his grasp.

Actually, he always cried. He had cried at the slightest provocation ever since the day he was born. The sharp, piercing sound would echo through our big old house and really irritated me, especially when I was working.

Being a historian, I spend a lot of time in my study at home. I inherited a large library of historical books from my father, who was also a historian. And since the library is next to my study, I rarely need to go anywhere any more. I did actually have a job once; I worked as a lecturer at the university, but when things started getting rough, I decided to quit the job and concentrate solely on my writing. There was a lot of unrest in those days – students were always protesting about this and that. Unrest is one thing I simply cannot abide.

Looking back, I'd only accepted the university post because I wanted to get into the university archives anyway. I had often written articles for historical publications, and having all those research sources at my disposal inevitably increased my output. But as soon as I quit the university post, I received a series of big commissions and my income rose significantly.

Of course, quitting the job didn't stop me using the university archives. I still go there once or twice a month to borrow books I don't have in my library. And, yes, I was on my way home from the university that day when I bought the albino toy monkey for my baby boy.

Some weeks after buying the monkey, I went over to the university as usual, and on my way home, I passed the same toy shop and peered in through the window. The army of dark brown monkeys had disappeared, but it didn't strike me as particularly odd at the time; I figured they must simply have gone out of fashion.

I hurried up the hill to our house. I had no particular reason to hurry, but going uphill always makes me walk faster.

We live in an affluent residential district not far from the center of Tokyo. Until just a few years ago, the area was full of big mansions like ours, and like ours they were all dark and dilapidated. They all had tall trees in their gardens; oppressively dense foliage shrouded the roofs and windows, making the mansions look even gloomier than they were already. This gave them an added air of unapproachability. Most of those gloomy mansions have been converted to desirable modern residences with brightly lit porches, broad verandas, terraces shaded by canopies, and beautifully manicured front lawns. Ours is the only house in the area that still retains that murky, antique air it had in my father's day.

When I married Miwa, I was thirty-one and she was twenty-six. It seemed only natural that our life together would start in my father's old house, the home I was brought up in, but Miwa found it hard to get used to at first.

"I hate living in this big old house, it gives me the creeps!" she said, and I couldn't help agreeing.

"Let's have it remodeled then," I suggested, "like everyone else."

I meant it sincerely enough, but I never did anything about it; there always seemed to be something more important to do. And as we grew accustomed to our new life in the house, Miwa started to complain less and less about it. Sure, she would let out the odd grumble on occasion, but on the whole, we slipped into a state of passive acceptance. And when the baby was born we had other things to occupy our minds.

Still panting from my exertions in hurrying up the hill, I pushed down the latch of our wrought iron gate. The gate, adorned with images of griffins and satyrs in the Gothic style, gave a metallic creak as it swung open. *Must oil those hinges*, I thought. A flagstone path leads from the gate to our front door, lined on both sides by cypresses, laurels, zelkovas, black pines and other gloomy old trees. The garden fell into neglect after the baby was born, and the path is now permanently hidden under a blanket of fallen leaves – even in summer. The wind blows leaves right onto our porch, making our old front door look more forbidding still.

I opened the door and called out to my wife. She didn't answer. I thought she might be in the living room or the kitchen, both of which are at the end of a long corridor. I called again, this time more insistently, but still no answer came.

157

I went into the spare room to the right of the corridor, put my briefcase down and peered through the open partition toward the living room at the back. Even in the dim half-light of late afternoon, it was clear that no one was there. *Must have gone shopping*, I thought. So I went straight upstairs to my study and got on with my work.

The murky gloom of twilight gave way to the dark silence of evening.

Miwa still hadn't returned. I started to worry and called a few people I could think of, but she wasn't with them. Her parents live hundreds of miles away in Kyushu; she couldn't just have hopped over there at the drop of a hat. My anxiety began to grow.

I sat vacantly in the living room and waited for her to come home. As I did, I started to think things over.

Miwa surely had no reason to leave me. True, it was becoming quite fashionable for people to vanish without a trace, but she had a baby with her. With no source of income how would they survive? Perhaps she'd been having an affair and had finally run off, taking the baby with her. But no – she wasn't that kind of person. Nor was she the type to commit suicide. She'd left no note, at least none that I could find; and in any case, I could think of no valid reason why she would do anything so drastic.

As I sat there in the gloom, I started to wonder whether I could find any clues to help solve the puzzle. I had a good look around the living room.

The only pieces of furniture in the room were a cabinet, a television and a low table. The baby's tiny futon lay in one corner with a pretty pink-and-green quilt flung loosely over it. On top of that was the baby's pale blue coat, which he always wore when Miwa took him out. On the pillow lay a pacifier and a white teddy bear; they too went everywhere with him.

Even with the lights on, the room still felt dark, and now it started to feel cold as well. I went to the kitchen to make some tea. Miwa's shopping basket was in its usual place on top of the fridge.

Suddenly, I heard the baby crying in the hallway. *They're*

back, I thought, feeling a momentary sense of relief – which very quickly turned to annoyance.

"Miwa! Where have you been?" I demanded angrily as I stepped into the corridor. But the front door was closed; no one was there.

Unable to bear the oppressive gloom, I switched on the lights in the corridor and hallway, then opened the front door and went out to the porch. The garden was wrapped in deathly silence under a moonlit sky. Zelkova leaves rustled softly as a gust of wind sailed past my face.

My ears must have been playing tricks on me; that was the only possible conclusion. I closed the front door, went back along the corridor and looked into the spare room just to make sure. All I could see was our old leather sofa and armchair, bathed in moonlight entering aslant through the window.

I went back to the living room and sat drinking my tea. As my eyes wandered vacantly over the baby's bedding in the corner, I suddenly noticed something: the toy monkey was missing. Then I remembered a strange incident from some days earlier. At the time, I'd written it off as some kind of delusion, but when I remembered it now, I really started to worry.

That day, I'd come to an impasse in my writing and thought I'd look in on the baby for a change of scenery. I went downstairs and peered into the living room. Miwa was in the kitchen. In the living room, the baby was sitting on the futon playing alone.

When I saw him, I couldn't believe my eyes. His right arm was missing – or rather, his arm seemed to gradually fade from the shoulder down, disappearing altogether near the elbow.

I rushed over and tried to pick him up.

He felt incredibly heavy, as if some invisible force was pulling on his invisible arm. But he didn't seem to be in any pain; he just stared at me blankly with his big, round eyes as if to ask why I was making such a scary face. He seemed completely fine, so I gathered all my strength and picked him up.

Now he suddenly felt lighter, and my momentum almost made me fall backward with the baby in my arms. It was as if

159

Yasutaka Tsutsui

someone, some unseen being, had been trying to pull him into a different dimension – a *vanishing* dimension– but had quickly let go when I started to pull him away.

Of course, the baby's arm was still there, just as it should have been. And the hand at the end of that arm was clutching the white toy monkey.

I thought I must have imagined it. My eyes had been tired, the room had been dark, and the baby's arm had been hidden behind him – all these had combined to create the illusion that his arm was missing. And having accepted the illusion, I'd convinced myself that his body would feel heavy. I didn't say a word about it to Miwa, as it was just too embarrassing to mention.

But now the memory of that weird experience returned, accompanied by intense anxiety. Had my wife and baby disappeared – *literally*? I began to feel agitated and didn't know what to do. Actually, there was nothing I *could* do. An image flitted across my mind: Miwa, surprised to find the toy monkey pulling our baby into the vanishing dimension, had desperately tried to help him and was eventually dragged into it herself. In that case, where could it all have happened? Here in the living room? I looked around the room again.

Ridiculous, I thought, shaking my head slowly. It was just a fantasy. How could something so absurd happen? The problem was this house, I decided: its oppressive gloom, its dimly lit rooms. It was the house that had conjured up those ludicrous delusions.

I got up from my chair. Miwa would come home; of course, she would. She would soon be opening the front door, trying vainly to hush the baby's constant wailing while apologizing profusely for her lateness. She would soon be standing in front of me with that hangdog expression of hers. There was nothing to worry about. Nothing at all.

Consoling myself with that thought, I went back upstairs to my study. I really had to get on with my writing, as the publisher needed the manuscript in a few days' time. Even if I couldn't finish it, I needed to show something half decent at least. It was already late enough.

But try as I might, I just couldn't concentrate; amongst all the papers and books piled up on my desk, I couldn't remember what was written where. I'd been working on a particular problem but had no idea which book contained the reference I was looking for, so I kept opening the same books in search of it, over and over again. It was a waste of time, but giving up was not an option. If I were to give up, I would have to face my solitude, my anxiety, not to mention my intense despair and irritation at being so incapable of doing anything for my missing wife and baby.

It was still no good; I couldn't even remember the problem I'd been working on. I got up and went to the library, where I would have to start again from scratch.

My library is cold and damp and smells of dust and old paper. It has four stacks more than two meters high, packed on both sides with books. Of course, the walls are lined with shelves, and those shelves are also packed with books. I pulled a book from a shelf by the wall and started to turn the pages as I stood there. Perhaps the reference I was looking for would hit me in a flash of inspiration.

Then I heard the baby crying.

I could hear it clearly. The crying stopped as abruptly as it had started, but my ears couldn't have been deceiving me this time. In the deathly hush of the library, there was no way I could have mistaken the sound for anything else, and I'd never had problems with my hearing before.

With the book still in my hand, I hurried past the ends of the stacks, peering down each narrow aisle in turn. The baby was nowhere to be seen, but when I reached the last stack I heard another sound behind me – the metallic sound of the white monkey smashing its cymbals together.

"Bang bang! Bang bang! Bang bang!"

I couldn't stand it any longer. "Miwa!" I called loudly as I retraced my steps. "Where are you? Answer me!"

About halfway down the central aisle, I saw the baby. He was facing away from me, but something wasn't quite right: he was floating about a meter off the ground, and his body had a vague,

161

hazy appearance. As I stood there in astonishment, his body started to shimmer like a mirage, then turned into something two-dimensional, like a thin piece of paper, drifted languidly toward the nearest bookshelf and started to disappear. It was as if something was pulling him in there. His body hovered in the air like a wisp of smoke before finally vanishing between two books. That was no mean feat, as the books were packed together tightly without the tiniest gap between them. It was like a film of someone smoking in reverse, making it look as if the exhaled smoke was being sucked back into the smoker's mouth.

This all happened in a fraction of a second. I ran straight to the spot where the baby had disappeared. Though knowing it would be in vain, I pulled out several volumes from the shelf where he'd vanished, hurled them down onto the floor, then pulled out the books next to them, then the next, throwing them all down on the floor in turn. I was frantic.

And, yes, it was all in vain. There was nothing behind the books – only the fore edges of the books on the other side.

I squatted on the floor and buried my face in my hands. All I could hear was the persistent banging of those cymbals. "Bang bang! Bang bang! Bang bang!" It seemed to go on forever.

"I must be going mad," I muttered. I had to say something, anything, it didn't matter what; if I hadn't, the oppressive silence of that windowless room would have been simply unbearable.

For the first time, I thought of calling the police to report my wife missing. Part of me knew it would be a waste of time; another part said it was the only thing I could do. I phoned the local station and gave the barest details to the desk sergeant, though naturally omitting to mention the mysterious happenings in the house. I didn't want anyone to think I was losing my mind. Speaking with deliberate calm, I explained that Miwa was unlikely to do herself harm. That seemed to satisfy the sergeant, who suggested I complete the formalities at the station the next day.

I replaced the receiver and returned to my desk. I wasn't hungry, though I hadn't eaten. Sleeping was out of the question.

Why had an apparition of my baby appeared in the library?

Why had I heard his voice? Perhaps he and my wife had disappeared in the library, not in the living room. But they never went to the library – why would they have gone in there? On the other hand, perhaps they were everywhere. Perhaps they were ghosts; perhaps they were both dead, their lifeless bodies hidden somewhere in the house.

The very thought made me lay my head on the desk in despair. My wife and baby were dead, and their ghosts were roaming around our gloomy old house.

I lifted my head again. How could I possibly think something as stupid as that? Ghosts don't exist! I had to keep my sanity. Keep thinking straight.

I peered out of the window at the old trees standing in our darkened garden. I could see the pale reflection of my face in the window, and beyond that, the eerie sight of cypress leaves swaying silently in the wind.

Suddenly, the image of Miwa holding the baby appeared in the dim half-light beyond the window pane, hovering outside amongst the swaying cypress leaves. The image was hazy and ever-changing, like a picture going in and out of focus. Just when it seemed almost transparent, it would take shape then just as quickly turn hazy again. At one moment it looked two-dimensional, as thin as paper, like the image of the baby in the library; the next moment it was three-dimensional and real again.

"Miwa!"

I leapt to my feet, slid open the glass door and ran out onto the balcony. Grasping the handrail firmly with one hand, I leant out toward them. They seemed to be floating in midair somewhere between me and some cypress branches just beyond the balcony. Their images were rippling, shimmering, like a film projected onto a moving screen. When I tried to reach out and touch them, my outstretched hand clawed nothing but night air.

The baby seemed to be crying, but I couldn't hear a thing. He was holding the albino toy monkey in one hand. Miwa was carrying him at shoulder height and had a look of fear in her eyes. She was looking around anxiously and seemed unable to see me.

"Miwa!" I shouted. "Miwa! It's me! Look, over here!"

She turned abruptly to look in my direction, her long black hair swirling around her pallid cheeks. It was as if she'd heard my voice for just a second, as if she'd seen me for the briefest moment. She seemed to be calling back to me; her lips moved, but I could hear nothing.

With the baby clutched tightly in her left arm, she stretched her right hand out toward me. At that moment, the image was no longer transparent but solid and three-dimensional. There was a sense of reality in her hand and white fingertips, stretched out until they could almost touch mine.

Suddenly, something brushed against my hand; it could have been Miwa's fingertips, but it could equally have been a cypress leaf fluttering down. Or it may just have been the wind rushing past.

I leant forward to stretch out my arm further. The albino monkey now took on a definite shape and started moving toward me, as if it had broken free from the baby's grasp. As it came closer, it started smashing its cymbals together.

"Bang bang! Bang bang! Bang bang!"

The noise began to reverberate in the dark. The images of my wife and baby grew more transparent and started to shake violently; they seemed to be fading to nothingness. I caught a momentary glimpse of despair on Miwa's face before they disappeared altogether.

"Bang bang! Bang bang! Bang bang!"

Only the toy monkey remained, hovering just a few meters in front of me. It continued to smash its cymbals together frantically and seemed to be making fun of me, but I could only stand there in stupefaction as I watched it. A chill wind blew through the night air as the toy monkey started to float toward me, banging its cymbals all the while.

When the monkey was within arm's reach, I stretched out and tried to grab its head, as if to snatch it from an unseen hand. To my considerable surprise, I succeeded in doing just that, and I now had the monkey firmly in my grasp. It stopped moving, but had its elbows spread wide, ready to smash the cymbals together again at a moment's notice.

"So, you're back," I muttered as I glared at the monkey. "And where are the other two then?"

Of course, there was no reply. As I held it in my hand, the monkey looked straight ahead with an air of innocence, as if to say it had nothing to do with those strange goings-on. But I was sure of one thing: the monkey had taken my wife and child into that vanishing dimension.

I looked around the room, half expecting their images to appear again from somewhere. What was it like in the vanishing dimension? Was it dark? Was it a world where everything was distorted and nothing had any depth, a world that could be three-dimensional at one moment and lacking in substance the next, like the images I'd seen of Miwa and the baby?

One thing for certain was that it was not the real world of the here and now, but existed on a different plane altogether. It was *another* world – not a *parallel* world. So what kind of world was it? Where was the boundary between these two dimensions, and where were the entrances and exits? Was there perhaps a passage leading between them? How could I find the passage and enter that world? And if I did manage to enter it, could I ever return to the real world?

I looked at the monkey again.

It's the monkey, I thought. The monkey was the only thing in the real world that could take me to the vanishing dimension. I gripped it tightly in my hand.

"Come on then," I muttered. "Take me there. Take me where you've taken them!"

I expected the same thing to happen as I'd seen before with the baby: my body would gradually vanish, starting with the hand that gripped the monkey. But what if I vanished and could never came back? The thought did cross my mind, but I banished it immediately. The monkey had come back, after all.

It had all seemed so real. Miwa had been looking for me, asking for my help. I couldn't have been imagining it; the look on her face was enough to convince me of that. But a curious thing was that the baby seemed to appear wherever I went. So perhaps that other world, that vanishing dimension, could be entered from anywhere in the real world – even from an enclosed space like my library. In that case, the other world was one that lacked a concept of physical distance, a world without dimensions or geometrical constraints.

What did it matter anyway? The important thing was to rescue my wife and child.

I stared at the monkey. It was still there, and so was my arm. Neither had vanished or even started to.

I waited on the balcony for what seemed an eternity; if I couldn't disappear, perhaps the other two could reappear. But they didn't. In the end, I went back inside with the monkey still gripped tightly in my hand. The wind outside had begun to feel cold, and mental fatigue had all but exhausted me.

Our bedroom is opposite my study, to the right of the stairs. I went in and slipped gratefully under the bedcovers, taking the monkey with me. I was determined not to let go of it, as I thought it might try to vanish while I was asleep. If it did, it could transport me to that other world to see my wife and baby – as long as I held it tightly in my hand.

As I started to doze, fragments of nightmares began to appear in my half-dreaming state. They seemed to be issuing a threat: if I were to fall into a proper sleep, far more terrifying dreams would come to torment me. The result was that I stayed half-awake most of the night. At one point, as I drifted in and out of consciousness, I noticed that I'd let go of the monkey. There it lay, motionless beside me. I opened my eyes wide in the darkness and strained my ears in the hope of hearing the baby's voice again. But there was nothing – nothing but silence – a deep, maddening silence that smothered me with despair as I lay in bed. And there I lay for what seemed a very, very long time.

Morning finally came.

I couldn't bear the dismal gloom of the house any more, so I decided to take the monkey for a walk.

Everything outside was exactly the same as always; the traffic on the road, the people on the sidewalk, the shops and buildings were just as they had been the day before. But to my eyes, the whole scene seemed somehow shallow, distorted, shimmering – unreal. Even the noise from the street sounded hollow.

I went into a café that had only just opened and was still empty. I ordered a strong coffee and sat by a window, where newly disturbed dust danced in gleaming shafts of morning sunlight. Even as I drank, I held the toy monkey tightly in my jacket pocket, for I was still in the real world, however dreamlike my surroundings were. As long as I held the monkey, I might find a way of breaking through to that other world, that unreal world where my wife and baby were imprisoned.

I finished my coffee and left the café. And there, out in the street, I could hear the baby crying. I stopped and listened hard.

There, even amid the clamor of the street, I heard it again. It was definitely the baby crying; it wasn't the noise of pedestrians hurrying past on their way to work; it wasn't the sound of car horns blowing. It was the sound of the baby crying.

The crying continued.

Suddenly, I felt something tugging at my right hand, which was still clutching the toy monkey in my pocket. I quickly took the monkey out and felt a slight resistance as I did. But there was nothing unusual about the monkey or my right hand. They were both there; nothing had changed. The difference was that the sound of crying stopped as soon as I took the monkey out.

The monkey had been trying to vanish, I was sure of it. It had been trying to pull me by the hand into that vanishing dimension, but I had stopped it by pulling it back into the real world. That was why the baby's crying had stopped; as long as the monkey remained with me in the real world, there would be no connection with that other world, and no sound would emanate from it.

But Miwa was following me; she was trying to communicate with me. That was why I'd heard the baby. She was following me wherever I went. She was calling for my help, constantly.

I was once again overcome by a terrible sense of anxiety. I had to do something.

Knowing it was a futile gesture, I went to the police station and completed the formalities to report my wife missing. The desk sergeant asked a few simple questions, which I answered as best I could, then I left the station and wandered aimlessly around the streets.

Eventually, I began to wonder if that was, in fact, the wisest course. If Miwa was following me, looking for me, I surely wasn't helping by moving about so much. Home was the best place to be. So I went back to the house just after midday.

The streets around our house were settling into their usual afternoon calm; the only sounds I could hear were the occasional car horn or the squealing of brakes on the main road. Even those sounds faded to nothing as I opened our wrought iron gate and started walking along the flagstone path through our gloomy overgrown garden. Shafts of sunlight shone down through gaps between thick layers of laurel and zelkova, dappling the undergrowth of boxwood and gardenia with patches of light.

I suddenly stopped in my tracks; I could hear the baby crying again.

It was coming from the direction of a large viburnum bush to the left of the path. At the same time, the monkey was tugging gently at my right hand inside my pocket. Keeping a firm grip on it, I stepped slowly through the azaleas toward the source of the sound.

When I reached the viburnum, the crying seemed to be coming from above my head, but there was no sign of the baby anywhere.

I sneaked a look at my right hand, still firmly buried in my pocket. I could feel the toy monkey in my hand, but could no longer feel the pocket. Looking closer, I saw that my right hand had disappeared.

I lifted my arm toward the viburnum bush. Though the bush was right in front of me, I couldn't touch it. Of course I couldn't – my hand was already in the vanishing dimension! My vanished hand, with the monkey still firmly in its grip, had disappeared into that unreal world, together with half of my arm. And that wasn't all; my arm was continuing to disappear, slowly, gradually, toward my elbow and upwards.

"Hello . . . ?"

I heard Miwa's voice above my head. I gasped and looked up.

"Hello? Are you there? You're there, aren't you?" her voice called in agitation. Sometimes it seemed more distant, sometimes closer, but it was still above my head. Could she sense that I was in the garden, or had she seen my vanishing right arm in the other world?

"I'm here!" I shouted. "Miwa! Where are you?"

"I don't know," she groaned hopelessly. "Everything's distorted. There's no sense of time here. I don't know how to explain. You've got to help me!" Now she was crying. "Help me, please help me!"

I raised my half-vanished arm high above my head. My right hand, still gripping the toy monkey, brushed against something in that unseen space; it felt like a foot. I was touching Miwa's foot in the vanishing dimension.

I was about to let go of the monkey and grab her ankle, but then I thought again. If I were to let go of the monkey, both she and the baby might cease to exist. The monkey might vanish altogether, and my wife and baby might never be able to return. Not only that, but my right arm might be permanently missing from the elbow down.

So I kept the monkey firmly gripped in my right hand while lifting my left arm high above my head. I tried to grab my right arm with my left hand, but there was nothing at all where my right wrist should have been; my left hand clutched thin air.

Next, I tried to grab the elbow of my disappearing arm. That I could do. But it was too late – my right elbow disappeared at that moment, and my left hand with it.

My left hand touched Miwa's foot in the invisible space, so I grabbed her ankle with my left hand and pulled hard. Her bare foot appeared in the space above my head, together with my previously invisible left hand. I gathered all my strength and pulled harder. It was difficult with just one hand, and the left one at that, but I pulled as hard as I could. First Miwa's shins, then her knees, then her skirt-covered thighs gradually appeared in the space above me.

Still grasping her ankle in my left hand, I stretched further up with my right arm, the invisible one that was holding the invisible toy monkey. I placed it around what I thought was Miwa's midriff, then grabbed her knee with my left hand and gave it another pull. This time her hips appeared, followed by her middle, together with the baby's little legs.

I then tried to pull the whole of Miwa's body down to the ground. I spread my legs, crouched and pulled with every ounce of strength that I possessed, but I hardly had any strength left. I started to panic. Both my wife and the baby had already reappeared up to their shoulders, and all that remained in the vanishing dimension were their heads.

I gambled everything and let go of the monkey, grabbed Miwa's waist with both hands and pulled her all the way down.

Their two bodies came crashing down on top of me. Miwa's feet had only been a few inches from the ground, so her fall was not too hard. I fell on my backside, and as I lay there on the grass, the petite figure of my wife, holding the baby to her chest, came tumbling down next to me.

I glanced at them and let out a cry of despair.

"It was too early!" I screamed. "I let go too soon! The monkey, I let go too soon!"

Miwa's head was missing, and so was the baby's. Their bodies faded into nothing from the shoulders up.

Miwa never got her head back. Nor did the baby. My headless wife now sits in solitude all day long, cuddling our headless baby in the living room, that room where it's perpetually gloomy even in the daytime. Of course, they never go out.

I can touch Miwa. I can hold the baby. But we can't talk, and I can't hear the baby cry. Miwa can't see me. When I go to take the baby from her arms, she momentarily resists and tries to pull him back. I tap her lightly on the arm to reassure her, and only then does she pass the headless baby to me. I feel pity for their plight, but there's nothing I can do to help them.

The albino toy monkey has disappeared altogether. Maybe it passed across to that other world, along with their two heads, never to return. Sometimes I hear the sound of the monkey's cymbals, just when I think I've forgotten about it. But the monkey has never shown its face to me from that day on.

Occasionally I hear snatches of the baby crying. Sometimes it's when I'm with them in the living room; sometimes when I'm alone in my study. Sometimes I hear it when I'm walking along the main road, and sometimes when I'm poring over the university's historical archives.

And once, just once, I saw their two heads floating in the air.

It was when I was in my study one night. My eyes were tired from squinting at books, and I wanted to take a rest. When I glanced out the window into the darkened garden, the ghostly faces of my wife and baby appeared in front of the cypress tree, just as they had done before. Miwa's eyes were closed. She was pressing her cheek against the baby's face; she must have been carrying him, but of course I couldn't see that. The boy was asleep, and looked so angelic. Together, they made a scene as beautiful as any Madonna and child. I was stunned. But perhaps it was only natural that they should look so beautiful – because their faces belonged to another world.

"There's no sense of time," Miwa had said of the other dimension. What had she meant by that? That there was no temporal dimension in the other world, that unreal world? If so, it might explain why Miwa has never seemed to age and my baby has never grown an inch from that day to this. A headless picture of eternal youth, Miwa spends all day, every day in our living room, in quiet solitude, perpetually holding our eternally babyish child.

I sometimes think she may have found happiness in that. After the baby was born, she no longer complained about living in our big, silent, gloomy old house. Even before these strange events occurred, she had already stopped going out or looking after the garden. For all I know this new lifestyle may be the one she really desires; at least it means she'll never have to go out again.

And maybe it's a kind of happiness for the baby, too – preferable, surely, to growing up with the burden of being an albino and going out into a world where he would face nothing but taunts and hardship all his life.

But one thing troubles me. What will happen when I die? My eternally young wife and baby will live on. They will have no need of food or drink, and no need of society. Even after I'm dead and buried, they will continue their endless life of solitude, holding each other tight, sitting in that gloomy living room at the back of our murky old house, as long as the house exists. Until someone discovers them there. . . .

Oh! King Lear!

The celebrated actor Shinichiro Tatei, a firm believer in tradition, was famous for his portrayal of Shakespeare's King Lear. He had even set up the Dento-za theater company to perform that play and none other.

Tatei's productions of *Lear* were not set in the present or in some post-apocalyptic future. They were not based on any modern re-interpretation, nor did they rely on innovative staging; the acting was purely classical. As a result, Tatei was seen as a bit of a dinosaur in the theater world.

Even so, he was still invited to perform at school arts festivals and drama master classes on a regular basis. In fact, he'd spent eleven years touring schools around the country with his *Lear* along with the twenty or so members of Dento-za – mostly young men and women who had been lured by Tatei's fame. What attracted them more than anything, though, was his insistence on realistic performance. They would happily learn specific acting techniques under Tatei's tutelage, only to find themselves endlessly performing the same part, week in, week out, with little hope of advancement. As a result, they would eventually lose interest and seek greener pastures.

But Tatei didn't mind; he was sure his former pupils would never forget him, even when performing different roles for different companies. When asked where they'd learned their art, they would talk about him. And so his name would live on.

King Lear had three daughters, Tatei only one. Her name was

Akiko. She too had been trained by her father – in the role of Cordelia, of course – but took the opportunity to desert him when her mother died. Akiko then joined a major theater company as its leading lady and went on to star in numerous movie and TV productions. Though sad to lose his Cordelia, her father could but watch with pride from afar.

Now Tatei lived alone but felt little inconvenience, for he was constantly surrounded by people who were more than happy to look after him. Some were actresses in middle age; another was a veteran actor who had helped to form Dento-za and was now the company's manager. All held Tatei in the highest regard. So too did the younger actors, who played various roles while helping with set design, lighting and other work behind the scenes. Until they lost interest, that is.

In fact, Tatei's cup overflowed in a number of ways. He still received occasional calls to appear in movies and TV dramas and gave lectures on drama twice a month at a university. That provided a modest living, with enough left over to pay the members a small salary.

But Tatei, now in his sixties, was starting to notice a decline in his creativity; he couldn't help feeling that his Lear was growing stale. There were, after all, only so many times he could perform the same role without it becoming mechanical. Yet he had lost any ambition to change his repertoire. At his age, a single mistake could spell disaster, so he would have had to work even harder to master a new part. With Lear, on the other hand, the occasional stumble could not only be forgiven – it was almost expected.

Unbeknown to all, Tatei had been searching for ways to spruce up his act for some time. He had toyed with various ideas, but the gimmicky styles attempted by other companies seemed shallow and superficial; it would have been unthinkable for an actor of his standing to mimic them.

Tatei was in a quandary, with no obvious solution. He didn't know what would come of it; perhaps nothing would. Nakai, the company manager and a long-standing friend of Tatei's, had noticed a change in him, and several of the other members sensed a difference too. But they weren't sure whether their concern was something they needed to worry about. Confusion and uncertainty reigned.

If only Akiko were here, Tatei thought from time to time. She would surely bring new inspiration and ideas – because she was his daughter. She shared his sensitivity, his values. Yet however hard he wished it, she would never come back. His desire to have her by his side was probably just a parent's egoism, he thought. Society would surely not have allowed such self-indulgent behavior from a renowned performer and intellectual.

To be fair, he had found a decent replacement for Cordelia. She was actually better at delivering the lines, but lacked Akiko's charm and underlying sincerity. Partly out of frustration with this, Tatei would occasionally cast his mind back to Akiko during performances of *Lear* – especially in Act III, Scene II, when Lear wanders the heath with shame in his heart, following the betrayal by his two elder daughters and his foolish disinheritance of the youngest, Cordelia. At such times, Tatei would recall fond memories of Akiko's acting style – her tone of voice when delivering her lines, her face, her voice – and would be overcome by unbearable emotion, almost like Lear himself.

Then one day, something odd happened. The company had been invited to perform at a school arts festival in northern Kanto. There, on the stage of the school hall, Shinichiro Tatei as Lear wandered half-crazed over the stormy heath in Act III, accompanied by the Fool. Suddenly, he heard music. Well, actually, it was the ringtone on a smartphone, but Tatei recognized the tune. Or, rather, he had a vague memory of hearing versions by Andy Williams and Frank Sinatra in the '60s. Yes, and there was a disco version by the Boys Town Gang in the '80s. The song always reminded Tatei of happier times; whenever he heard it, he would think of Akiko while singing it to himself, changing the lyrics to suit the situation. The ringtone played the instrumental break, and when it finished, Tatei promptly burst into song:

I love you, baby! Come back to me tonight,
You're daddy's baby, come back and make things right.
I love you, baby, trust in me when I say:
Oh, pretty baby, oh how I miss that day.
Come back to Daddy, I wish you'd come to stay
And let me love my baby, let me love you. . . .

Tatei stopped in his tracks and stood dumbstruck on the stage, hardly able to comprehend what had happened. The play had been going so well, and he had ruined it. The Fool was rooted to the spot; the Earl of Kent, waiting in the wings for his entrance, just stood there open-mouthed. Tatei had done something utterly unforgivable.

For a moment, the pupils in the audience watched in stunned silence. Then they started to clap. At first halfheartedly in twos and threes, then with more enthusiasm, until in the end, they were giving him a standing ovation.

The commotion eventually died down, the play resumed, and Tatei returned to his normal performance of Lear. He could do so because, though not exactly filled with joy that his little turn had been so well received, the reaction reassured him that he hadn't totally disgraced himself. And, if anything, the other cast members supported him with even more impassioned performances than ever. Greatly relieved, Tatei could immerse himself in the rest of the play with his customary vigor.

After a rousing curtain call, the teacher in charge of the arts festival stood facing the stage. "Thank you so much," he said. "That was great. As an encore, would you do the song again? I'm sure our boys and girls would love to hear the song again."

Tatei could hardly refuse. And so it was that he reluctantly sang all of "Can't Take My Eyes Off You" in front of the closed curtains.

After most performances, the cast and crew would go to a pub near their hotel, or, if there was no pub nearby, back to the hotel restaurant, where they would sit at a long table and hold a post-performance meeting. Actually, it was really just an excuse to have a few drinks. That evening they went to a pub, where the discussion inevitably revolved around "the song" and various opinions were proffered.

"For a moment, I thought you'd gone mad," said Nakai, who played Gloucester. "I was a quivering wreck back there!" The others laughed raucously. Some of them had certainly thought the same thing.

"Actually, I could go with it," said the young actor who played the Fool. "After all, at that point Lear is already half-mad anyway. And though he doesn't say so, he's thinking of Cordelia, regretting his treatment of her. So the song fits the situation perfectly. Let's do it every time!"

"No, no," Tatei retorted with uncharacteristic bashfulness. "That would not be permissible for an actor in classical theater."

"We always ask people to switch their phones off. It's only good manners after all," said the veteran actress who played Goneril but also handled the announcements. "But maybe it wasn't such a bad thing at all. I mean, we might never have heard Mr Tatei's wonderful singing if it hadn't been for that ringtone. So, if anything, we ought to be grateful! And it showed our commitment to contemporary theater. An old-school actor would have been completely thrown by it; if we were doing a comedy, he would have made a joke about it. I think Mr Tatei's reaction was perfect."

They all agreed with that.

"I had no idea you could sing so well," said the Fool.

They all agreed with that as well.

"Well, of course, any actor worth his salt should be able to sing," said Tatei, feigning modesty.

"Please do the song every time," said the young actor who played Cornwall as well as taking care of the sound effects. He had a look of rapture on his face. "It brought tears to my eyes, it really did. We're in Kanagawa next, right? There's a band I know. I'll get them to make a karaoke track. Maybe you could do the whole song."

No, that would be a bit much, one of them said, but again they all agreed in principle. And the more Tatei resisted the idea, the more persuasively they pressed their case. In the end, Tatei acceded to their demands just to get them off his back. Against his better instincts, he reluctantly agreed to sing the second half of the song, the part after the instrumental break; he would sing it at the same point in the play and for one performance only. He knew he would have no trouble making up the lyrics, as he was doing that all the time anyway.

Tatei sang live during King Lear #whatevernext, one of the boys in the audience had tweeted. It went viral. The school in Kanagawa received so many applications for tickets to the next performance that it had to set aside half of the Culture Center for public seating. The performance was a roaring success. Now, even for Tatei himself, the song was no longer a sideshow; it was getting far too serious for that. He agreed to make it a regular part of the production and rehearsed it with his usual rigor.

Normally, when a published song is used on stage in Japan, royalties have to be paid to an organization called JASRAC. But seeing as this is just a short story by Yasutaka Tsutsui and the original lyrics haven't been used that much (and what's more, nobody actually sang the song), perhaps we can forgo that formality.

Which is just as well, really, because the song turned Dento-za's production of *King Lear* into a smash hit; the royalty payments would have been astronomical. Audience numbers grew with each performance, newspapers asked for interviews, and TV cameras were brought in. Akiko even called, saying she'd cried when she saw the news on television.

As time went on, the song assumed ever greater importance in the production; if anything, the play itself was becoming a sideshow. Then some of the actors started saying it was a shame to restrict Tatei to just one song. Couldn't he squeeze in a couple more? Some even wanted to perform a song themselves, but Tatei wasn't so sure about that. The most enthusiastic in this regard was the actress who played Cordelia. She admittedly had a good singing voice, but her suggestions were all recent hits. "A load of rubbish, can't understand a word they're singing," as Tatei put it. No, no, no, he said. Classical theater is about delivering the lines. Songs with such garbled, nonsensical lyrics would be unbecoming for a production by Dento-za.

The actor who played the King of France had more or less gleaned Tatei's inclinations. "Why don't I sing a duet with Cordelia?" he suggested. The song he proposed was "Smile", originally composed by Charlie Chaplin as the theme for *Modern Times*. Tatei knew the version by Nat King Cole and was not entirely opposed to the idea. In fact, he thought it would be fairly easy to write some new lyrics and find a place for the song in the play.

"But the King of France is never alone with Cordelia. When would they sing it?"

"I know!" said one of the younger actors. "Why don't we write a new scene, one in which only the two of them appear? After all, the King of France is besotted with Cordelia, so he could come to console her after she's banished by Lear."

The others agreed.

Tatei once more bowed to the majority view and agreed to add a new scene. He had some trouble working out the lyrics, but in the end a second number was added to the company's production of *King Lear*.

Tatei's preference for old-fashioned songs was now clear, and soon various other suggestions started to emerge.

"Talking of Chaplin," said another young actor, "how about 'La Violetera', the theme song for *City Lights*? It could be performed by Goneril and Regan when they hatch their plot at the end of Act I."

This idea was not so well received. "Out of the question," said Tatei. "Having two villainous characters singing such a cheerful song would undermine the whole meaning of the play."

Then the veteran actor who played the equally villainous Edmund made a strong pitch of his own. "Let me sing 'Misty'," he said. "You know, the one composed by Erroll Garner and performed by Ella Fitzgerald?"

"And Sarah Vaughan, and Nat King Cole. Of course I know it. It's a song of the highest caliber and, as such, impossible to master."

"I'm sure I could master it. I have every confidence. Let me try!"

Tatei could hardly refuse out of hand, given Edmund's status as the main character of the play's parallel plotline. If Lear had a song, why shouldn't Edmund have one too?

"Well, 'Misty' would be quite appropriate, I suppose. A song with an atmosphere of mystery. . . . We could use it to replace Edmund's long malevolent monologue at the beginning of Act I, Scene II."

"Couldn't we do both?"

"No. That would make the play too long. We'll have to cut the text to make room for the song."

Predictably enough, the young actor who played the Fool now asked if he could sing a few numbers of his own – not full-length songs but short bursts or ditties that would let him show off his vocal prowess and versatility. As chance would have it, the Fool already had a few bursts of song in the play as it was. With some reluctance, Tatei allowed him to sing just two more – "La Violetera," which Tatei didn't dislike, and "When You Wish upon a Star," the theme song for Disney's *Pinocchio*. These would be performed in Acts II and III, respectively, and once again, the Fool's lines were cut to accommodate the songs.

To use these songs on stage, the company should normally have paid exorbitant royalties to the aforementioned JASRAC, but since this is just a short story by Yasutaka Tsutsui and they were all fictional characters, they were free to use them as they pleased. Herein lies the freedom of the fiction writer. Oh dear. The author has interrupted the story just to eulogize the freedom of the fiction writer, a deviation quite unbefitting a work of fictional realism. Will he ever be forgiven?

"All right, that's enough. No more songs," announced Tatei. Dento-za's *Lear* was starting to be regarded as a musical, and for that very reason, in fact, the production had been booked for a whole month's run at a major commercial theater in central Tokyo. Pandering to the audience was not Dento-za's style and contradicted everything Tatei believed in.

But there were other members of the company who had a talent for song. The middle-aged actor who played Kent wanted to sing in Act IV, which didn't have a number of its own yet. Tatei refused, as Acts IV and V were the climax of the play and songs would just be a distraction. Kent was not at all happy to hear that. Dissent was also brewing amongst several other actors who wanted to sing. Tatei couldn't help feeling particularly strong rancor from Goneril and Regan, who had seen their idea for "La Violetera" stolen from them by the Fool. Sometimes they expressed their resentment openly at post-performance meetings. *Alas! I'm just like Lear*, thought Tatei, *surrounded by enemies on all sides.*

As the songs increased in number, so too did requests for shows – so much so that Nakai had trouble coordinating the schedule. This had never happened before. And as each of the singing actors gradually mastered their songs and honed their performance, the resentment of the non-singing actors inevitably grew.

The month-long run in Tokyo was approaching fast, when suddenly, rebellion broke out at one of the post-performance meetings. To Tatei, at least, it was clearly a rebellion – hatched by Goneril and Regan, he was sure.

Goneril lit the touch paper. "This play is so depressing, so unremittingly bleak," she said. "Perhaps we should all sing a happy song at the curtain call." At first, Tatei didn't pay the slightest attention to the idea, thinking it was a bit late to call the play bleak. But to his astonishment, the suggestion was heartily backed by all – even those who had no confidence in their singing and had never once asked for a song of their own.

To Tatei's greater astonishment, Nakai fell in with them too. "The ending is bleak, that's for sure," he said. "We've had high school students saying it made them cry all night long. It's probably too hard for people of this generation to understand.

After all, they're used to happy endings these days; they want therapeutic drama, not this kind of grim allegorical stuff."

"So you want to negate the world constructed in this play by singing at the end?" snorted Tatei, shocked by his friend's disloyalty. "Exactly what are you proposing we sing then?"

"'It's a Small World'," Regan declared without hesitation. The conspirators had obviously planned it all in advance.

Tatei could hardly fail to know that song, since it blared almost everywhere in mobile ringtones and the like. He was aghast at the idea; astonishment didn't even start to cover it. "Hang on, hang on, hang on! 'It's a Small World'? Why on earth would the world of *King Lear* be a small world? It's an affront to Shakespeare! Why, why, why, when the curtain goes down on *Lear* do we all have to traipse off to Disneyland? Are you all insane?"

"But it is a good song," piped up a voice, to which all once more agreed.

Tatei had no beef with that pronouncement. The song was, after all, written by the brothers Robert and Richard Sherman, composers of many Disney tunes.

"Perhaps we could look at it this way," said the actor who played Edgar. He couldn't sing for toffees, but his acting ability was unquestioned. "At the end of the play, everyone is down because the conclusion is so gloomy. But then we're saying, look, even this world of King Lear is nothing more than a small world; it could all have turned out differently. Instead of this dismal ending, Lear could actually have made friends with the other characters and turned it into a fun world. That could be our message to the audience."

"But why a small world?" Tatei retorted loudly. "Why does Great Britain have to be a small world?"

"It's a small world *today*," said Goneril. "Have you not heard of globalization? If we all sing this happy song at the end, the audience will be instantly transported from that sad, depressing world to the small world of today. I think they will all be moved by it."

For once, Tatei was speechless. The others all looked down at the table in grim silence. Clearly, they were not about to give way; clearly, they all thought success would be guaranteed if only *King Lear* could end in a song. Tatei sighed aloud before reciting a line from Act III: "Nor rain, wind, thunder, fire, are my daughters. I tax not you, you elements, with unkindness."

Oops! We seem to have inadvertently quoted from the script of *King Lear*. Still, seeing as this is a work of fiction by Yasutaka Tsutsui, and since Shakespeare is out of copyright anyway, perhaps we can get away with it again.

Tatei's little outburst, delivered perfectly in character as he would have done on stage, signaled to the others that he was about to concede. They had expected it anyway; some chuckled with satisfaction.

"All right. Do as you please," Tatei said at length. "But take care, as the Tokyo run is approaching fast. Someone will have to write the lyrics quickly, and there isn't much time. Rehearse, rehearse, rehearse. We have five members who can't sing. Make sure you can all do it."

Opening night in Tokyo was a roaring success. The audience was taken aback at first, as no one had any idea "It's a Small World" would be performed at the curtain call. But eventually the applause kicked in, and in the end it was to whoops and cheers that the curtain came down for the last time. The song sent out the childlike message that the world portrayed in *King Lear* must never be allowed to happen, that instead we should create a world where everyone is smiling and happy in mutual friendship. Yet it even struck a chord in the discerning minds of intellectuals, precisely because it was so unlike anything they would ever have expected from Dento-za. The newspaper reviews were favorable, too; "A breath of fresh air," said one. "Just what this play needs," another.

Tatei, who had opposed the idea so vehemently, couldn't help but be amazed at the play's success. Of course, he felt too awkward to show his joy openly to the other company members; instead, he remained resolutely sour-faced long after each performance had ended. Yet even he would soon know happiness beyond

Yasutaka Tsutsui

compare, for as he prepared himself for another evening on the boards, a knock came on his dressing room door. He opened the door to see Akiko standing there. "I'm back," she announced, beaming broadly.

Meta Noir

I seemed to be playing a role much younger than my actual age. Most of the scenes had already been shot and only a few remained. I was in a corridor dimly lit by sunlight streaming through a distant window, assisted by indirect lighting. As I passed the door to the secretary's office, she came out and stopped me. The secretary was none other than the popular actress Kyoko Fukada. She was about to give me a message from the company president, and, in the process, reveal her concern about him. Kyoko's skill at playing a devious career woman surprised me; I had known her since we appeared in an idol movie together more than ten years earlier.

"Kyoko, your acting has really improved," I said candidly, going off script to speak my mind. She responded by sighing loudly and looking up at the ceiling, as if she had just remembered something. My tone seemed to remind her of times gone by.

"Ah, yes. It was *School Days of the Dead*. I was eighteen and it was my first lead role in a movie – you played the villain. Then there was *Millionnaire Detective*, which you wrote. Yes, we've done quite a lot together, haven't we *sensei*?"

"Please don't call me *sensei*," I said, taking care not to be overheard. "I'm an actor in this one."

"My! So you have limits after all," she said with a smile before returning to the script. "Anyway, would you please call in at the president's office? He seems quite down about something."

"OK."

I left Kyoko Fukada in the corridor and went for a smoke in the green room before reporting to the president's office. The green room was not a dressing room but a company meeting room. That is to say, it was a set that could be used as a meeting room. I had to wait there because they wanted to take two more shots of Kyoko Fukada in the corridor before shooting the scene with the president.

The assistant director finally came to call me, so I made my way to the president's office. The president was played by Soichiro Kitamura, veteran actor of countless TV dramas. He sat at a desk with his back to the window; it was daytime outside. "You wanted to see me?" I asked, and he looked up from the papers in front of him.

"Ah, it's you," he said, on script, then started moaning about things in his usual dreary tone. He was really cut out for the part. I'd known him ever since he played the lead in my stage plays *Star* and *March Hare* thirty years ago.

He went on to tell me his thoughts, though still in character as the president. "Dramas like this have been all the rage recently, particularly since the nuclear accident at Fukushima. You know, companies on the verge of bankruptcy, dithering bosses, employees up in arms, and in this movie, some oddball taking potshots at the president. Ahahahaha!" It was a convoluted story; a bleak movie in which each character had some kind of dark secret.

"Have you been killed yet?" I asked, still acting the role of the subordinate.

"It's tomorrow. I'll be killed about this time tomorrow. No matter how often I do it, I still hate being killed. It makes me think about life, you know? Well, *my* life at least. Ah, that reminds me. It probably won't come to this, but should anything happen to me," he said, suddenly returning to the script and taking an envelope from his desk drawer, "please give this to the police. It could be the last thing I ever ask of you. Ahahahaha."

"I hope not," I said, but took the envelope all the same. "So tomorrow's your last day? I'm not needed in that scene, so I

186

probably won't see you for a while. And there's no wrap party this time."

"That's right." The president hunched over slightly and peered up at me. "So long then."

I normally took a taxi home, but on that day a location minibus had been arranged. The vehicle slowly edged its way past tourists in the narrow back streets of Harajuku before arriving outside my residence.

As I approached the sliding wooden gate in front of my house, I could see the front door opening on the other side. "Hello, dear," my wife called as she came out, and how surprised I was to see that it was the actress Yoshiko Miyazaki. I know her reasonably well, as she played Satomi Ishihara's mother in *My Grandpa* and, like me, belongs to the Horipro talent agency.

"Oh! So you're playing my wife in this one?" I asked without thinking. She smiled.

"It's just a cameo," she replied. "I didn't get much warning."

She seemed to be playing a wife who frets over her husband, for she suddenly adopted a worried frown as she returned to the script.

"Are you all right, dear? You had that strange phone call this morning, didn't you. Has something happened at work?"

"No, no. Everything's OK. It's nothing important." The scene wasn't in the original script, so I just came out with the normal platitudes I would spout when talking to my wife.

"Really," she said, looking unconvinced as she withdrew to the back of the house. I went straight upstairs to my study without taking my jacket off. I was reading through some e-mails on my desktop when my wife came in. This time it was my real wife, which surprised me again.

"What, you mean you're appearing in this movie too?" I asked.

"I don't appear in movies," she replied disinterestedly before extending an arm and placing an envelope on my desk. "You've a letter from Mr Oe." And with that she left the room.

A letter from Kenzaburo Oe, with the characteristic upward slant of his handwriting on the envelope. I picked up a paper

187

knife to open the letter but hesitated to use it, for I knew that if I were to read the letter, I would want to reply immediately, as I always do. If I had done that, I would have been myself; I would have been an author. And that would have been out of keeping with my role in this movie. As I continued to vacillate, a voice came from a corner of the room.

"Go ahead, read it," said the director, squatting next to the camera there.

This guy's got a nerve, I thought with some dismay at the director's lack of manners. I opened the envelope and read the letter nonetheless. The director seemed to think he'd captured enough of my private life with that, so he made a suggestion.

"Hey, the crew are going back on location to prep tomorrow's scene with Kitamura and the yakuza mob. I'm finished for today, so how about grabbing something to eat somewhere?"

With this director, *somewhere* is always the same place: a sushi bar in Kagurazaka.

"You mean Umegae?"

"You got it."

I went to the kitchen, where Yoshiko Miyazawa and my real wife were standing and chatting. I told my two wives I wouldn't be needing dinner, then headed for Kagurazaka in the location minibus with the director.

As it was quite early, Umegae was still empty. It's about the size of a hotel room and is run by three sushi chefs. We sat at the counter facing the head chef, an old acquaintance of ours. As we gobbled hand-pressed sushi swilled down with *shochu* on the rocks, the director and I discussed the movie. This was the first time we'd spoken alone together.

"To be honest, I'd prefer to be seen as an actor," I said, a little inebriated already. "Some directors just assume that because someone is a writer they can't be any good at acting. They're like teachers putting on a school play. That just kills my motivation, as I never get any decent parts. I'm glad you trust me in that respect, at least."

"No, no. You've really helped by taking part in this movie.

But, of course, the other actors also need to understand that it isn't just a pile of garbage." The director narrowed his eyes as he did when admiring an actor's work. "Thanks to you, the style of this movie has started to show, which is strange when you consider what kind of movie it is."

"No, no, no. It's because you understand metafiction. There are plenty of directors who understand literature but not many who could be so avant-garde as this, though, of course, some reviewers will still call it a pile of garbage," I said with a chuckle.

"Oh, sorry," said a voice at the back of the restaurant. I turned to see the camera assistant behind us. "Sorry. I need to change the film."

"What? You're filming here too? No wonder the chef was looking nervous!" I gave the director a quizzical look. "OK. How you're recording the sound is anyone's guess. But you're actually appearing in the movie yourself? That really is going a bit far."

"What do you mean?" the director laughed. "How could I not film such a tasty scene as this?"

Naturally, he wasn't referring to the sushi. But as I didn't seem too happy and he probably thought I couldn't speak freely now, the director decided to call it a day. "OK, it's a wrap," he said, turning to the camera assistant. "Forget about the film. Get your ass over here and have some sushi." I wondered why he'd only brought the camera assistant, armed with nothing but a handheld camera. Maybe he thought I would make some "tasty" remarks.

The next day was my day off, but I didn't feel like doing other work while the movie was still being shot. After my one-day break, I arrived on set just after lunch for the final scene. Eiichiro Funakoshi was already there; he was my scene partner for the day. The set was a large company office with about thirty desks lined up in neat rows. It was a night scene, so it was dark outside. Lights from a cluster of office buildings outside created a beautiful backdrop. I wondered if the movie really warranted such investment in visual effects, but I assumed it must have been because the director wanted a strong finish. I stood facing Eiichiro Funakoshi, who was seated. We had already appeared in a number of mystery dramas together, with him in the lead role. We talked briefly in a corner of the office. It was way past office hours, so there was no one else in the room.

"They'll be filming the final scene now," said Funakoshi. "After that, they just want a few shots of me walking here and there, sitting in trains, that kind of thing."

"That's a lot of work," I said. "It must be hard playing the lead all the time."

The camera was already starting to roll, but I got another shock when I glanced at the director standing next to it.

"What the hell happened?!"

I approached him with deliberate nonchalance; after all, he was also appearing in the movie. His face was covered in bruises. In fact, hardly any member of the crew was without some injury or other.

"Well, yesterday's session was a real corker, I can tell you," he said gleefully. "I asked the yakuza guys to ad lib some lines, and they just ended up punching each other. It was a complete free-for-all. I tried to intervene but got caught up in the action instead." He laughed, and I noticed that his front teeth were missing. "And so did the whole crew!"

Was there any limit to this director's nerve? "And did you film that too, the scene where you tried to intervene but got punched instead?"

"Oh yes. How could I not film such a tasty scene?"

"And was Kitamura all right?"

"Sure. No problem. He'd already been killed, so he'd gone home."

I went back to my original position in the scene. Eiichiro Funakoshi looked up at me from his office chair.

"I can't get used to the rules in this movie," he said. "Or should I say the *rule:* the rule that there are no rules. I'm trying to understand it, but I just can't."

"It's no better when you're used to it," I replied, not understanding too well myself. "The director seems to be filming everything – including our confusion about him filming everything."

"Yeah, I bet he's filming this as well," Funakoshi said with an air of resignation, but then returned to character. He was glad the incident had been resolved, but still didn't know why it had to happen. Those were the last lines in the script.

"By the way," I added as an afterthought, "we're near the end of the movie now, so you must have been killed already. Or should I say, *almost* killed. You didn't die because you had some kind of rare illness, but that hasn't been explained yet, has it?"

He looked momentarily perplexed as he thought about it. Then he looked up at me again.

"The subplot was mentioned once, in an earlier episode."

"Oh? I wonder if audiences will remember that." I turned to the director to convey my misgivings. "Is it really going to finish like this?"

"You bet," he replied, showing his missing teeth in a grin. "You just said we're near the end of the movie, didn't you?"

"You call this a movie?" I exchanged looks with Funakoshi and gave a wry smile. "It's just a pile of garbage!"

"Final shot!" the director suddenly called with an air of fresh resolve. "You two walk out. We might not use it, but just ad lib some parting crap."

"Well, I must be going," Funakoshi said as he got up from his chair.

"Me too. I'm exhausted."

We walked out through the double doors, which had been left open. The director kept the camera rolling even after we'd gone out. The assistant director was checking a monitor in the corridor, and we stopped to look over her shoulder at it. All we could see was the empty office – no sound, no movement.

After a while, the final credits started rolling over the scene.

"Hey, what a cool ending!" said Funakoshi, grabbing me by the shoulder.

My eyes were glued to the monitor. "Yeah, and who knows? This could end up winning awards!"

The Agency Maid

My wife had been in hospital nearly a week when the agency maid finally arrived. I was relieved more than anything, as I'm completely useless at housework and can't even feed myself properly. I'd heard about the agency at the hospital and had phoned them on the very first day, but had been told they were short of staff at the time. So I had no option but to go to the hospital every day and complain to my wife about the inconvenience of it all. Hardly ideal behavior when visiting a loved one. The nurse had finally lost patience, saying my wife's condition would only get worse if I kept moaning at her.

"Good morning, Mr Muraki! I'm from the agency!"

The voice on the intercom sounded young and full of energy. I opened the door to see a petite woman, in her late twenties or so, with a smile so wide that it filled her whole face. The impression she gave was one of boundless charm.

"I'm Maki Yamaguchi," she gushed. "Pleased to meet you!"

I welcomed her in, resisting the temptation to flirt.

"What should I call you? Miss Yamaguchi? Ms?"

"Oh! Just call me Maki!"

So that was what I did. She asked what kind of food I liked; she asked for three thousand yen. Then off she waltzed to the shops, singing a song I didn't recognize.

I went back to my studio and got to work making little wooden chests and brush stands. That's what I do for a living.

193

Before too long, Maki came back with the shopping and started busily preparing dinner in the kitchen.

"Muraki-san!" she called at length. "What time do you want to eat?"

"Whenever it's ready, thanks."

"Any clothes to wash?"

"Only what I've put in the machine."

"Want anything else done?"

"Not right now."

"Can I bin the old food in the fridge?"

"Please do."

So the conversation continued on either side of my studio door. It was oddly enjoyable, though I felt a bit guilty when I thought of my wife. The dinner was a selection of my favorite things, with some others thrown in; I wasn't too keen on the simmered eggplant, but I was in no position to complain. While I ate, Maki made the next day's breakfast, then put it in the fridge before going home shortly after seven.

The next day, I visited my wife as usual. When I told her about Maki, she smiled faintly. "I see. So you like her, then?"

At first I thought she might be jealous, but her expression showed no sign of that at all. The radio next to her bed was playing the song Maki had been singing the day before. I guessed it must be pretty popular.

My wife had chronic myelogenous leukemia. She had been treated for it once before, but the condition had returned. The doctor said her prognosis was very poor; she might even die. If that were to happen, I would have been utterly helpless.

That day, Maki had come to the house just after midday, her normal time, and had tidied up my studio while I was at the hospital. I was happy with that, as all my materials and work tools were now neatly cleared away in their proper places.

As she was getting ready to go shopping for dinner, I made a suggestion. "Why don't you get enough for yourself as well? We could eat together if you're not in a rush."

"No, there's no rush. That would be nice. Thank you!"

She said she would normally grab something at a convenience store as it was too much bother to cook just for herself. So that evening we ate dinner together in the dining room while chatting about this and that. Maki said she was single; she couldn't find anyone to marry.

"That seems hard to believe," I said. "Someone as nice as you. Why ever not?"

"No idea!" she said with a breezy laugh, as cheerful as ever.

Several days went by in the same way. I would visit my wife in the morning, and when I got home Maki would already be there. I would do some work in the afternoon, then we would eat dinner together. And after she had gone home, I would do some more work, have a drink and go to bed. Every day was the same.

One day, I worked later than usual and kept Maki waiting until eight o'clock. I decided to have a drink with my dinner as I wouldn't be going back to work afterwards.

"I think I'll have a drink this evening," I said. "How about you?"

"A drink? Oh . . ." She rolled her eyes for a moment then gave a decisive nod. "You mean wine? I think I could manage a small glass."

So we drank wine. It soon made her tipsy, in a cute kind of way. We chatted about the world, movies, elderly welfare. I enjoyed it so much that I was starting to get carried away – and Maki laughed in all the right places.

"Why don't you stay?" I suggested. It was already after eleven, and she was beginning to look quite drunk; she was swaying from side to side and her gaze was straying.

"Ah. Oh. No, I couldn't." Maki glanced at the clock, looked up at the ceiling as if in despair, then slumped down in her chair. "How did it get so late?"

"You could sleep in my wife's bed. It's too late for the train."

"I can still make it."

"You shouldn't, not in your state. It's my fault. I shouldn't have let you drink so much."

"No, no. I could have stopped."

The alcohol suddenly seemed to have gone to her head. She put her hands on the table, stood up unsteadily, tried to walk away then lurched to one side and flopped down on the sofa in front of the television.

"You can't sleep there."

"No, no. Here's fine. I'm good." And she fell asleep.

I fetched a quilt from the bedroom and draped it over her as she lay fully dressed on the sofa. The relaxed expression on her face made her look quite angelic; I stood momentarily transfixed at the sight.

For some reason, I felt agitated that night and couldn't get to sleep. My heart raced at the thought of a young woman asleep in the dining room, and though I felt bad when I thought of my wife in the hospital, I enjoyed that feeling immensely.

The next morning, after waking earlier than usual and feeling slightly aroused, I was surprised to find that Maki had already left. Maybe she'd felt ashamed about staying overnight in a married man's house; maybe she couldn't forgive herself for it. Whatever the case, I felt a twinge of regret.

I decided to change my usual routine and wait for Maki to come at her normal time. But her normal time came and she still hadn't arrived. It was now past noon and I was getting worried; perhaps the agency had suspended her for staying overnight at a client's house. In that case, I would have to apologize, as it was my fault. So I decided to phone the agency.

The phone was answered by the woman I'd spoken to previously. "Oh, hello," I said, "My name's Muraki. Miss Yamaguchi hasn't arrived today. Is something wrong?"

"Yamaguchi?" said the woman, sounding confused. "We don't have anyone called Yamaguchi."

I was at a loss for words; it didn't make any sense. I babbled incoherently before ending the call, got dressed right away and headed for the hospital. My heart was thumping. The hospital was only two stops away on the local train, but in my state of agitation I decided to go by taxi.

My wife's ward was on the third floor. As I stepped out of the lift, I sensed an unusual air of commotion and started to fear the worst. As soon as my wife's nurse saw me, he came hurrying in my direction.

"I just tried to call you," he said. "It's your wife. She's critical."

By the time I got to her ward she had already lost consciousness; her face was as white as a sheet. She was on life support but would never be herself again. With tears in my eyes, I went close to her and gazed at her beautiful face. "Thank you," I said quietly. "Thank you so much. It was you, wasn't it? Maki Yamaguchi was you."

The Night they Played Hide and Seek

Why did Tetsu and the others stay behind at school that day? Maybe it was their turn to tidy up the classroom. No one else stayed behind that day; no one but Tetsu and the others.

It was already late afternoon when they started playing hide-and-seek. Before long, twilight set in and the corridor lights began to flicker on. The classrooms were dark and quiet. That made playing hide-and-seek even more fun.

Children shouldn't play hide-and-seek at night. Something bad always happens when they do. That's what they'd always been told; they all knew it. So why did they play hide-and-seek so late that night? And that night, of all nights?

It must have been because it was even more fun than usual. That was why they couldn't stop. The boy who was 'it' would put his head down on the teacher's desk and count to a hundred, then he would start to look for the others.

Once, when Tetsu was 'it', he put his head down on the teacher's desk and just went to sleep.

"Tetsu! Tetsu!"

Someone was tickling him under the arms, trying to wake him. It was Matsu.

"Ah! I found you, I found you! I've found Matsu!" shouted Tetsu.

None of the boys knew what time it was any more; they were

all enjoying the game of hide-and-seek far too much to notice. It was completely dark outside. Looking out of the windows, they could see the moon shining high in the night sky.

Now Gen was 'it'. Tetsu looked for somewhere to hide. In the end, he went to the library, where a single light shone brightly in a corner. Tetsu gazed at the bookshelves, so tightly packed with books. Suddenly, he noticed a book he'd never seen before.

Tetsu-chan loved reading; he had read most of the books in the library already. The book he found that night was *Mysteries of the Cosmos*. The teacher in charge of the library must have brought it in that day. Tetsu took the book out, sat at a desk and started reading it under the bright light in the corner.

And he forgot all about the game of hide-and-seek.

That's how interesting the book was. All the things that had puzzled Tetsu until then were explained in the book. It satisfied his curiosity. As he continued to read it, he discovered a lot of new things that puzzled him even more. And when he had finished reading the book, he couldn't remember why he'd stayed at school so late.

Tetsu hurried home, and from that time on, he read a lot of books about space. Tetsu was just his nickname; his real name was Tetsuo Yamamoto. Ever the good learner, he eventually went to university and studied astrophysics. His decision was probably influenced by the book he'd read in the library that night.

Tetsu immersed himself in his studies. After graduating from university with a first-class degree, he stayed on to study some more. He discovered a lot of things and became a professor of physics.

One day, Tetsu suddenly remembered the night they had played hide-and-seek. It filled him with a warm sense of nostalgia. And then he realized he'd become so engrossed in *Mysteries of the Cosmos* that he'd completely forgotten about the game of hide-and-seek. Tetsu felt really bad about that; he felt sorry about letting the others down. They had probably forgotten about it, but the memory must have been retained, somewhere at the back of their minds.

That year, there was a primary school reunion. Tetsu decided to go, as he'd never been to anything like that before. In the evening, after the reunion was over, Tetsu went to a bar for a drink with his old classmates. As they were drinking and reminiscing happily about old times, Tetsu realized that the classmates in the bar were the ones who had played hide-and-seek that night.

"Remember the night we played hide-and-seek?" he asked the others.

They all remembered. And they all realized the same thing – that the classmates who had played hide-and-seek that night were all together in the bar.

"We never finished that game of hide-and-seek, did we?" said Matsu.

Matsu was an actor's son. Following in his father's footsteps, he had taken the stage name Matsuzo Ichikawa; now he was quite well known.

"Hey, that's right! We never finished it!" they all replied as one.

"Gen was 'it' at the end, wasn't he?"

Gen's real name was Genichi Hisanaga; he was a journalist now. Everyone called him Gen-san, and he was very popular.

Gen immediately put his head down on the table for a few moments. Then he looked up, pointed at each of them in turn, and called out their names.

"Tetsu – found you! Matsu – found you!" And all the others. They all laughed aloud.

"Oh dear. You found us all in one go."

"So who's going to be 'it' next?"

Everyone except Gen played rock-paper-scissors to decide who would be 'it' next. Tetsu was the loser, so he put his head on the table and started counting. Gen, Matsu and the others giggled as they crept out of the bar in ones and twos.

After counting to a hundred, Tetsu lifted his face. No one was left in the bar. Now Tetsu giggled too. Then he paid the bill for everyone's drinks and went home, still giggling.

Gen worked as a journalist for many years until at last he

retired. One day, he read some sad news in the newspaper: the famous actor Matsuzo Ichikawa had died. According to the article, Matsu had been good friends with Tetsu until the day he died. Someone at the newspaper must have known about their friendship, as Tetsu had been asked to write an obituary.

In the obituary, Tetsu wrote about the night they had played hide-and-seek. He also wrote about the time they reminisced in the bar after the class reunion. At the end of the article, Tetsu wrote: "From that time on, Matsuzo often came to visit me in my university laboratory. It was always after he had finished performing, so it was usually quite late at night. But that was all right, as I always work late anyway. Once, when I was feeling tired from my studies, I had rested my head on the table and was taking a nap. Then Matsuzo crept up next to me, tickled me under the arms and said, 'Tetsu! Tetsu!' I woke up to see Matsuzo's smiling face. 'Ah! Matsu,' I said. And I wished we could go back to that game of hide-and-seek all those years ago."

When he read that, Gen wept openly.

Overcome with a feeling of nostalgia, Gen went to see Tetsu in his laboratory that night. It was already dark, but Gen knew that Tetsu always worked late. He knew it because Tetsu had said so in the obituary.

Gen made his way to the Physics Department and found a door marked "Tetsuo Yamamoto, Professor of Physics". The university was deserted, but Tetsu was still in his laboratory, surrounded by piles of books.

Tetsu had rested his head on the desk and was taking a nap. Gen crept up next to him and tickled him under the arms.

"Tetsu! Tetsu!"

Tetsu woke with a start.

"Ah, Gen. I found you," he said.

Their eyes instantly filled with tears. They were so overcome with happy memories that they hugged each other and cried like babies.

After that, they talked long into the night about Matsu and

things that had happened in the past. They were talking about the night they'd played hide-and-seek, when Gen suddenly remembered something.

"You remember the night we played hide-and-seek? There was a boy we didn't know very well. Remember?"

"That's right. There was!" Tetsu also remembered, gasping in surprise. "He was a new boy, wasn't he?"

"Yes. His family lived near my house," said Gen.

"He wasn't at the class reunion, was he? What was his name?" Tetsu tried to remember. He had a faraway look in his eyes. "That's right. I remember now," he said at last. "It was Fukuda. He told me when I was 'it'. I found him hiding under the stairs. I said 'Ah—!' and pointed at him, but I couldn't think of his name, so he smiled and said, 'Fukuda'. His name was Fukuda."

Now Gen also remembered. "That's right! It was Fukuda! But why was he playing with us so late?"

"Well, he'd just changed schools. He probably wanted to make friends."

"Ah. This takes me back."

"Yes. Me too."

The two said nothing for a while as they wallowed in nostalgia.

"But then why didn't he come to the class reunion?" Gen said with a puzzled look. "And why didn't anyone notice he wasn't there? After all, there were eight of us when we played hide-and-seek but only seven in the bar."

"Are you sure?"

"Yes, I'm certain."

Tetsu slapped his knee. "Maybe he still thinks we're playing hide-and-seek? Maybe he's still hiding there, somewhere in the school building!"

Gen opened his eyes wide. "Could he be?"

"Of course! Think about it. We haven't seen him since that day, have we?"

Gen agreed. "All right, why don't we go back to the school and look for him?"

"Yes. Let's do that."

Tetsu and Gen promised to go back to the old school together, one day.

But they never kept that promise, because Gen suddenly fell ill. It wasn't a very serious illness, but he was bedridden for a long time.

One day, Gen heard that Tetsu had died. "So," he thought, "I'll never find Matsu and Tetsu now." He remembered the game of hide-and-seek. He remembered that he was 'it' now.

Gen regretted not going back to the school with Tetsu; he regretted not going back to look for the new boy who had disappeared. He regretted it until the day he died.

The Countdown Clock

I was in Oddo's clock shop again.

The shop wasn't always called Oddo's; in fact, every time I went there it was called something different. But some things were always the same. Like the old-fashioned interior with its collection of strange and wonderful clocks. Or the cantankerous old watchmaker with his rimless spectacles.

"Here I am again," I said, doing my best to sound friendly.

"Huh. You again," the watchmaker grunted, as if it was too much trouble to greet me. "What do *you* need a clock for? You're not interested in the time of day. Not in your profession. And you hardly ever go out these days. So why do you keep coming here?"

"I'm not interested in the time of day, true, but I am interested in timepieces," I replied with a smile as I peered into a glass case next to his repair table. "So. Got anything unusual today?"

The watchmaker eyed me sternly over the top of his glasses. He reminded me of an old acquaintance of mine, a musician. He also looked like a man who used to work in the local post office when I was a boy. Sometimes he resembled various other people I knew; he was a kind of grumpy alter ego inside my head. And, of course, that was why he knew me so well.

"Well, there's this one," the watchmaker said as he took out a watch and held it up. "The minute hand goes round in forty-five minutes and the hour hand in nine hours."

The watch face only showed the numbers one to nine.

"And when would that come in handy, I wonder?"

"Never. That's why it's interesting."

"Yes, that is interesting," I agreed. "The fact that it never comes in handy is interesting. And what other interesting timepieces do you have today?"

The watchmaker took out another watch that didn't look at all unusual. "This one was inspired by a story in a magazine. The Needle, it was called."

"So what's special about it?"

"At the stroke of noon, a very fine needle comes out of this tiny hole at the back, sticks out about three millimeters then zips back in again."

"Doesn't it hurt?"

"No, it doesn't. The wearer just feels a very slight pricking sensation. It leaves no mark. You put deadly poison on the tip of the needle and give it to someone you want to kill."

"So it's the perfect crime. Excellent. What else do you have?"

The watchmaker stared at me. "You've been here countless times before, haven't you? In your dreams? You've already seen all the strange clocks and watches in this shop, even this one. I must have shown it to you long ago."

"So you did." I ran my hand over a clock on top of the glass case. "Ah, this one brings back memories. Wasn't it the Clock of Life?"

"That's right."

The clock face was embedded in a lump of bluish-black rock.

"And why was it called Clock of Life again?"

The clockmaker didn't answer right away but leaned slightly toward me. "You wrote about this in a novel twenty years ago. It was all right then, but you'd better not write about it now."

"Eh? Why not?"

"Because your readers will get emotionally involved, and then they'll be drawn into your subconscious."

"That's what I want them to do! What's wrong with that?"

"Everything. Unlike twenty years ago, you're too obsessed with death these days. It's understandable – people around you are dropping like flies. First your father, then your brother, then other writers, artists, musicians, your contemporaries. That's why you write about nothing but death in your short stories and novels. Even now – look!" he said, pointing at the street outside. A friend of mine, a famous cartoonist who had recently died, waved as he walked past the shop window.

I gave an exaggerated sigh for effect. "Well, of course, that does happen in dreams, but sometimes it happens when you think you're awake, too. You see someone you know and you can't quite remember whether they're dead or alive, don't you find? Sometimes, I even catch myself thinking someone who's still living, someone whose name I can't remember, is actually dead."

"There you are – that's proof you're getting obsessed with death. It's dangerous. I think you'd better not come here any more."

But the clock shop was one of the most important places in my dreams; even on my very first visit, it was already full of warm memories. So now, after so many decades, I could hardly imagine *not* going to the clock shop.

I looked the watchmaker in the eye. "In your dreams," I said, "you see some people as being dead, others as being alive, don't you? It takes time to work out whether someone you think is dead is actually dead in reality. It's a bit like a half-broken clock that sometimes works and sometimes doesn't, don't you think?"

The watchmaker gave me a dubious look. "Listen," he said, "a dead person is not a broken clock."

Sometimes I would find the shop after turning a corner in Ginza. Sometimes it was down a back street in Kobe. If I was in Osaka, I would find it along Mittera Street in Shinsaibashi.

And now I was in Kiddo's clock shop once again. The name was different, of course – it was always different. This time, I said nothing to the cantankerous old watchmaker but merely observed him at work while I stroked the Clock of Life on the glass case beside me. About a dozen books of different sizes were lined up on a shelf at the back. One of them was a thick, expensive-looking foreign tome.

"Is that a book about clocks?" I asked at length.

The watchmaker looked around at the shelf. "This one?" he said. "No, it isn't a book about clocks; it *is* a clock."

He took it off the shelf, laid it on top of the glass case and opened it. The open page showed a clock face set to a certain time of day. He turned to the next page; it showed another clock face set to one minute after the previous one.

"It's just a book. Why do you say it's a clock?"

"Well, look. It's a clock, isn't it? Time passes when you turn the page."

I smiled. "True. You've never shown me this one before."

"Haven't I?" the watchmaker said with a pensive look. "In that case, your way of thinking must have changed."

I took my hand off the Clock of Life and stared at him. "So there must be some other clocks I haven't seen yet."

The watchmaker groaned and stared back at me.

"There are, aren't there?" I said with a triumphant smile. "Some more weird clocks or watches?"

The watchmaker opened a drawer in his desk and started rummaging around. "All right, have I ever shown you the Countdown Clock?"

"I don't think you have."

"Well, here it is."

He took a folding alarm clock out of his drawer and placed it on top of the glass case. It was a digital clock, showing the time in six digits, but unlike other digital clocks, the time shown was not advancing; it was running down, and at quite a worrying speed.

"Hmm. That's unusual. What's it for?"

"It shows how much . . ." The watchmaker stopped in mid-sentence; the rest was just inaudible mumbling. Maybe what he said was unclear because it was a dream. You know? When you know what the other person is saying but you can't quite make out the words? Or maybe the shock would have been too great if I'd heard him clearly. I immediately understood what he meant, anyway. It was a clock that showed how much time I had left. That sounded familiar; why yes, only that very day I'd been wondering whether such a clock could actually exist.

"You'd best not convert the number to years," the watchmaker warned. "Just look at it casually, that's my advice. Don't think about it too much, then you'll feel OK because there seems to be a lot of time left. If you convert it to years, the shock might be too much for you."

"So where's the button to reset the time?"

The watchmaker grinned. "Button? What button?"

A sense of foreboding started to well up inside me. The watchmaker must have noticed it, as he suddenly frowned and snatched the clock from my hand. "No, no, no, no, no! You were going to break it, weren't you? No way! Twenty years ago you went berserk about some trivial thing and smashed this whole place up. I'm not going to let you do that again. It's one of your bad habits, losing your temper like that."

"Oh, come on! That was twenty years ago. I've mellowed since then." I forced a smile as I frantically tried to control my temper.

"Don't make me laugh. You will always be you. Who do you think you're kidding? No. Take a look at this."

The clock book was still lying on top of the glass case. On the open page, the hands were spinning around madly, though still maintaining the correct relativity; the minute hand was spinning twelve times faster than the hour hand. I turned the page. The hands on the next page were spinning around at the same mesmerizing speed.

"See? The clock's gone wrong," I said. "Come on, wake up. Wake up!"

I woke up without really wanting to.

It was never my intention to go to the clock shop in my dreams; if it had been, I would probably have never made it there. In any case, it was rare for me to remember the shop when I was awake. What usually happened was that I remembered it after I'd started dreaming, and only then would I want to go there.

That night, I found the shop down a back street in Ginza. It was called Eddo's clock shop this time.

"Could I see that clock again, the one you showed me before? The Countdown Clock?"

The watchmaker gave me a withering look. He was sitting at his repair table eating his lunch. "Can't you see I'm eating my lunch?"

"And is your lunch a clock, too?"

"No, my lunch is not a clock. It's my lunch. Though once I've digested it, I suppose it'll be part of my body clock."

I smiled.

The watchmaker finished eating and handed his plate to a small woman who emerged briefly from the back room. Then he opened his drawer and took out the Countdown Clock.

"Don't be too surprised," he said ominously.

The number on the clock face had gone down to five digits.

"Five digits? Isn't it a bit early for that?" I asked. "Just as I thought. It's a trick, isn't it?"

"No. It's not a trick, I assure you," replied the watchmaker.

"All right, I'll buy it."

"You're in a dream. You know you can't buy things in a dream," the watchmaker said, shaking his head. "You want to smash it to pieces, don't you? No chance. No way."

I thought I had it firmly in my grasp this time, but before I knew it, the Countdown Clock was back in the watchmaker's hands.

I promptly lifted the Clock of Life from its position on top of the glass case.

The watchmaker's face changed color. "What are you going to do with that?" he asked nervously. "There's your bad habit coming out again. Calm one minute, hysterical the next!"

"I want to see what's inside."

"You mean you're going to break it? Save yourself the trouble. Look. It's nothing but a little clock embedded in rock. See?" The lenses of his rimless spectacles had turned red.

"So why is it called the Clock of Life then? And why are you in such a panic about it?"

"All right. If you must know, it's not just a clock; it's your life

210

embedded in the rock. And that's not all. . . ." The watchmaker's face lengthened until he resembled an old mountain goat.

I had already opened my hands to release the clock. It fell to the floor and smashed into smithereens at my feet. Bluish-black fragments flew out of the fathomless depths of the rock and scattered over a square meter of the floor, together with hundreds of glittering particles of metal and glass from the clock. When I squatted down to take a look, I saw that they were all tiny clocks; each one was like an old pocket watch – an analogue watch with a face about five millimeters in diameter.

"Wow! That's scary! What's this supposed to be?"

"Now you've gone and done it." The watchmaker loosened up and started to speak more casually. "Well, you see, each of those little pieces was a clock belonging to someone you care about. That's all. Some of them are working, some of them aren't. See? The ones that aren't working belong to dead people."

"Some of them are working, then stopping, then working again. What are they?"

"People you dream about. You don't know whether they're dead or alive." The watchmaker's speech began to break up, then his face started to fade, until he eventually disappeared altogether. ". . . no . . . perception . . ."

The inside of the shop grew darker. I could no longer see where the walls met the ceiling, only countless clock faces floating in the air like departed souls. I felt a breeze on my back and turned, instinctively knowing that someone had come in. It was my old friend, the famous cartoonist who'd recently died. On previous occasions, he had just walked past the window and waved, but this time he pushed the door open and walked in with a broad smile on his face.

"Oh, dear!" he said. "Did you break it, then?"

"So you've actually come in this time, have you? It must be hard enough just walking past the window!"

"Why do you say that?"

"Well, you have to appear in a lot of people's dreams, don't you?"

The cartoonist laughed genially. "Go on with you! Who do you think I am, Santa Claus?" He bent down and, without a moment's hesitation, picked up one of the tiny clocks. "Ah! This is mine. Look. It hasn't stopped, has it? It doesn't keep stopping and starting. No, it's still working perfectly. Does that mean you think I'm still alive?" He smiled uncertainly.

"What gets me most," I said, "is dreaming of people whose clocks sometimes work and sometimes don't. It makes me realize there are people I've even started to forget about in my dreams. That really gets me down." I looked up at him. "Tell me something. Do you think dreams are fiction?"

"I think perhaps they're both fiction and reality at the same time. You once wrote that dreams are another reality, another fiction. Remember? That's correct, but there's more; sometimes they're a place for communing with the other side."

"Oh? Really?"

"Yes, really. Dreams are where I meet characters from my cartoons; I talk to them there. They're all interesting characters, sure, but since they're really just part of me, I do sometimes get tired of them," the cartoonist said, laughing again.

"Wonderful," I said. "That really is wonderful."

"But there must be people you only meet in your dreams, like the owner of that clock shop."

We were suddenly walking up a hill in a residential district.

"Now you mention it, places like this hill only ever appear in my dreams. Maybe we'll meet some of those people here."

Just as we came to a crossing, I saw a thin man crouched at the foot of a garden wall. He was dressed in long white rags and had a white hood over his head.

"Him!" I exclaimed. "Is he still alive? I haven't seen him in ages."

When the man saw us he shrieked like an old woman, covered his bruised face with one hand and peeped at us through his fingers, then started to crawl across the road.

"Oh no! You saw me!" he moaned as he went. "You mustn't see the face of one as unclean as I. No! I mustn't be looked upon! Ah!

I've been looked upon," he cried feebly as he wriggled along the ground. On reaching the other side, he crouched down behind a utility pole. He seemed to feel genuinely aggrieved, though enjoying his little act at the same time.

"Is he always like that?" asked the cartoonist, looking on in astonishment.

"Yes. He always does that."

The cartoonist laughed heartily then stooped to look me in the eye. "Isn't that interesting? Isn't that interesting?" he said, then laughed once more.

He seemed to be someone who knew everything.

We continued up the hill, walking side by side, until we came to the edge of a steep precipice. I always ended up on that precipice, but the route I took there was always different. It would usually be quite a complicated route and would serve to wake me up, but tonight I seemed to reach the precipice with the greatest of ease.

Maybe it's because I'm here with him, I thought as I eyed the cartoonist from the side. He was gazing down at the night view of the residential area spread out below us. Surprise was etched on his face, for the whole scene was filled with brightness; lights in the streets and houses below stretched far into the distance, as far as the horizon, where they merged with the stars in the night sky.

"Weren't you scared of heights?" the cartoonist asked with a puzzled look.

"Not here. I'm fine here. It's too high up, you see? It's like looking down from an airplane when you're coming in to land. No, I find it quite reassuring, actually."

I felt as if I was enjoying quite a philosophical discussion with the cartoonist as we stood on the edge of the precipice gazing out at the light-filled sky. But I only *felt* that way; in fact, I wasn't actually sure what we were discussing. That itself was proof that I was starting to wake up.

Before I knew it, I was back in Oddo's clock shop – alone. I must have gone there in a panic just before waking up. The watchmaker was nowhere to be seen; the Clock of Life was back in its usual position on the glass case, with the Countdown Clock sitting next to it. I had a feeling the watchmaker had put it there deliberately. I picked it up and looked at the time.

It was down to four digits.

Animated Realism

The counter of the bar is undulating and contorting as far as the eye can see. Antelopes, zebras, gorillas, wolves and foxes sit chatting with gazelles, lynxes and marmosets at the counter, turning their heads from side to side as they rise and fall with the movement of the counter. Some are literally howling with laughter.

The metal legs of my barstool keep twisting and bending, making it hard to sit straight. I cling to the counter to stop myself from falling. The bartender sees that and smiles but looks slightly worried. His face is broad and fat like a Halloween pumpkin. But no! Now it suddenly grows longer and turns into a cucumber.

Liquor bottles lined up at the back of the bar are all jostling for attention, desperate to show me their various shapes and colors. As each bottle in turn feels my gaze, it comes forward, swells up, then shrinks back and withdraws, only for the next one to take over. Each bottle proudly displays the label showing its country of origin and sings its national anthem by way of introducing itself. A Negro woman, a wild turkey, Catherine de Medici, they all sing. A silhouetted gentleman tap dances with a pirate captain. A buffalo and a swan race off together. Mexicans in sombreros play guitars while women holding roses dance the mariachi.

I can't remember how many I've had tonight. My highball glass slides back and forth with the movement of the counter as if it's trying to avoid me. I can't be bothered to catch it any more and decide to go home. I take my leave of the bartender, but he doesn't seem to hear me; he's too young to be going deaf, I think. I try to get off my stool, but when I look down, the floor is too far away. The gap must be ten feet or more. I'm sure to fall if I get off the usual way, so I grip the bar and carefully lower one leg at a time.

"Hey, you're not driving home in that state are you?" the bartender says with a smile.

What a strange thing to say. How else will I get home? Now the bartender has two heads on his shoulders – that must be why he's saying strange things. My feet are on the floor now, but the carpet suddenly starts to move like a treadmill, and I can't stand still. A bullfrog and a poodle sitting at a table come crashing into me, along with the table.

"Hey! Watch where you're going!"

When I say that, the poodle looks flabbergasted. "Speak for yourself!" she barks.

The door at the end of the passage is four or five hundred feet away. The floor keeps moving toward me, making it harder to reach the door. The door shakes its head and turns from side to side in front of me; it wants me to give up and stay in the bar. When I try to grab the handle, the door comes crashing into me. It hits me on the nose and makes me groan.

The bartender comes out from behind the counter. "Say," he calls, head swaying like a Chinese lantern at the end of his elongated neck, "are you OK? Can you get home on your own?"

"You need to change this door," I reply. "Get one that treats your customers properly."

The bartender doesn't understand. Yes, now I'm sure he's going deaf.

"You take care now."

I remove myself from the crazy distorted bar with the bartender's words echoing behind me. What's he so worried about? Take care of what? He can't be telling me not to drink and drive – that wouldn't make any sense at all. He must be dumb as well as deaf. Ha! My mind has never been clearer than it is now. I've never felt more in control; I'm on top of the world. Street lamps and lights in shops and restaurants seem to celebrate with me, shining radiantly as they approach me then move on by. Ah, but no. The lights are the glittering necklaces and earrings of beautiful women gathered here around me.

Filled with a sense of euphoria, I laugh aloud as I kick a plastic bucket that happens to be in the way. The bucket, about the size of an oil drum, rolls over on its side. The empty back street is as wide as an airport runway. I walk a few hundred yards along it before at last reaching the bar's private car park; it's the size of a football stadium. Along the sides, giant turtles, lizards and beetles all turn to look at me and start nervously rocking their bodies up and down. Hey, guys! What's to be scared of? The asphalt surface of the car park starts billowing up in giant waves, gathering in the distance before rushing toward me one after the other. This is not like normal asphalt – more like a soft carpet. I have to crouch low as I walk. I'm not going to let those piffling waves knock me over. Who do they think they are? Keep back. Keep back, I say!

Riding on the asphalt waves makes me feel a bit seasick. I stagger to keep myself upright, but I'm still feeling on top of the world. Oh! There's my lovely little one. My little white Rumba. Oh look, she's smiling, my cute little Rumba. You're always waiting for me. You're not like those nagging women with their "What time do you call this then?" You're comfortable to ride in, not like those vulgar women who keep writhing about and yelling their heads off. Ah, you look so happy. You're dancing up and down with joy. But, hey, don't overdo it, or I won't be able to open the door!

And in I get. Ah! Such soft and comfortable seats. They make me feel like taking a little nap. Ah, but no – must get home.

Hold on. What's this? Come on, stop messing about. Let me put the key in. Hey! Stop moving the keyhole around. Do you hate my key so much? Don't make that horrible face like Munch's *The Scream*! I'm OK, I tell you! I'm not drunk, I am not drunk. Jeez, you're beginning to sound like that bartender. But that's fine. I need you. I can't get home without you. So come on.

At last the engine starts. As I grab the steering wheel it goes

Yasutaka Tsutsui

all soft and floppy, like one of Dali's clocks. It even wriggles from side to side for good measure. The steering column expands then shrinks, comes toward me then moves further away. My eyes are starting to spin. What's that all about? Nah, it's OK. I'll be all right when I'm on the road. But I can't remember how to work this thing. Which pedal next? Accelerator? Brake? Which is which, anyway? Never mind. I'm used to driving, so it'll come naturally. Of course, it will. And bingo! We're moving. Ahahaha! We're moving. Ahahahahahahahaaaa!

I'm hemmed in on both sides. Can't turn with you lot in the way! Damned turtle. Get outa my way. Wahaha. I hit it. Dah, quit your hollering! Quit your screeching! Wahahaha. Goddamn dog in the way. Massive thing. Can't swerve. Just hit it, then. Ugh! What a noise. Both eyes smashed. Heh heh. But now the car park gives me the undulating carpet treatment again. Dammit. Eyes are spinning. Whole car park's rotating. Animals are doing a round dance outside. Must get outa here quick.

Stars look blurred and watery tonight. Red stars flash, green stars fade; purple stars come up to my nose. Flattened people line up on both sides, closing in on me, making me feel like I'm suffocating. Some of them have graffiti written on their bodies. Some are like great big arrows hovering over the ground. A blue moon comes up to the windscreen and smiles. And was that a rat? Big black thing with white lines on it, scuttling slowly across the front of the car. Spooky or what.

Now I'm in a desert, or some kind of wide-open space. Tent poles criss-cross in front of me; a camel train plods along beside me. A newspaper article flashing red and yellow cascades down like a waterfall, all the way down to the undulating carpet, where it breaks up. Big square eyes shine as they look down on me. Here and there, brightly lit screens show women standing motionless in different poses. The face of a hideous roaring beast appears large on a TV screen overhead. Herds of wildebeest move slowly forward around me, lighting up their red backsides as they go. For chrissakes get a move on! I yell, but they don't seem to hear. I know – I'll give them a beep. BEEEEP! Wahahaha. Now I'll do it again. BEEP BEEP BEEEEEP! Wahahahaha. Oh, diddums, they're getting angry.

Ah, now I can move. Go on, run! Run, my little Rumba, run! Wow, I never knew I could go this fast just by keeping my foot down. What a feeling! Like an adrenaline rush. I've gone beyond the sea of neon, and now I'm racing through the stars in the night sky. Racing. Galloping. Running. Running. Forever running!

Huh? Everyone's going the wrong way. Like they're trying to escape from something. Ah, now I see. It's rushing toward me. Some kind of monster with eyes wide apart. Or a giant turbanned Indian. Tuh! What's so scary about that? Look, I've put him in a panic. Serves him right. Oh, you want to have a crash, do you? All right then – bring it on!

The counter of the bar is undulating and contorting as far as the eye can see. Antelopes, zebras, gorillas, wolves and foxes sit chatting with gazelles, lynxes and marmosets at the counter, turning their heads from side to side as they rise and fall with the movement of the counter. Some of them are literally howling with laughter. Hang on. Where am I? This is the bar I left just moments ago. What am I doing back here?

The metal legs of my barstool keep twisting and bending, making it hard to sit straight. I cling to the counter to stop myself from falling. The bartender sees that and smiles calmly. His face is broad and fat like a Halloween pumpkin. But no! Now it suddenly grows longer and turns into a cucumber. He's dressed entirely in white. Wait a minute – everyone in the bar is dressed entirely in white. Even I am dressed entirely in white.

Liquor bottles lined up at the back of the bar are all jostling for attention, desperate to show me their various shapes and colors. But hey – they're all white. As each bottle in turn feels my gaze, it comes forward, swells up, then shrinks back and withdraws, only for the next one to take over. Each bottle proudly displays the label showing its country of origin, and the labels too are white. Characters and animals on each label sing national anthems by way of introducing themselves. And,

219

of course, they are all white. The Negro woman has a black face but is dressed in dazzling white; the wild turkey and Catherine de Medici are both completely white. The tap dancing silhouetted gentleman and pirate captain are exceptions: they're completely black. The buffalo is white, the swan naturally so. The Mexicans in sombreros and the women dancing the mariachi are all white. Even the roses dancing with them are white. What the hell is going on? Has the world suddenly turned monochrome? Or have I gone back in time, back to the days before full-color animation?

But I'm happy here. The bartender nods and smiles. Everyone smiles at me. Filled with a sense of euphoria, I laugh aloud. Wahahahahahaha. Who would have guessed such a place existed. I should have come here a long time ago.

First bo●k publication information

Bullseye!
ペニスに命中, from 世界はゴ冗談 (2015)
Call for the Devil!
悪魔を呼ぶ連中, from 笑うな (1980)
The Onlooker
傍観者, from 如菩薩団 (2006)
It's My Baby
産気, from 笑うな (1980)
Zarathustra on Mars
火星のツァラトゥストラ, from ベトナム観光公社 (1973)
Having a Laugh
世界はゴ冗談, from 世界はゴ冗談 (2015)
The Good Old Days
団欒の危機, from わが良き狼 (1973)
Running Man
走る男, from わが良き狼 (1973)
Sleepy Summer Afternoon
睡魔のいる夏, from あるいは酒でいっぱいの海 (1979)
Cross Section
セクション, from 笑うな (1980)
Narcissism
ナルシシズム, from 心狸学・社怪学 (1975)
Sadism
サディズム, from 心狸学・社怪学 (1975)
The Wind
風, from 串刺し教授 (1988)

A Vanishing Dimension
    母子像, from 革命のふたつの夜 (1974)
Oh! King Lear
    リア王, from 繁栄の昭和 (2014)
Meta Noir
    メタノワール, from 繁栄の昭和 (2014)
The Agency Maid
    つばくろ会からまいりました, from 繁栄の昭和 (2014)
The Night they Played Hide and Seek
    かくれんぼをした夜, from エロチック街道 (1984)
The Countdown Clock
    近づいてくる時計, from 最語の伝令 (1996)
Animated Realism
    アニメ的リアリズム, from 世界はゴ冗談 (2015)

The author

Yasutaka Tsutsui, born in Osaka in 1934, is Japan's pre-eminent writer of metafiction. Over the last six decades, he has produced dozens of novels, hundreds of short stories and numerous other works of literature, many of which have won national acclaim. Among others, he won the 1987 Tanizaki Prize, the 1981 Izumi Kyoka award, the 1989 Kawabata Yasunari award, and the 1992 Nihon SF Taisho Award. His latest and probably last full-length novel *Monado no Ryōiki* won the Mainichi Art Award in 2017. Though a cult hero and well-known TV personality, Tsutsui lives virtually incognito in Tokyo's bustling Harajuku district.

The translator

Andrew Driver, born in Oxford in 1954, has been translating Japanese for nearly three decades. He is a former resident of Tokyo, where he kick-started the Hysterick Theatre project and featured in the radio drama Woody's Week in the 1990s. In 2005 he conceived, compiled and translated *Salmonella Men on Planet Porno*, the first English-language collection of Tsutsui short stories, followed by the novel *Paprika*.

The artist

Youchan Ito was born 1968 in Aichi Prefecture, Japan. She launched her career as a graphic designer in 1988, becoming a freelancer illustrator in 1991 and founding Togoru Co., Ltd. with her husband in 2000. She handles a wide range of genres including cover art and design for science fiction, mysteries and horror titles, as well as illustrations for children's books.

www.youchan.com

Printed in the USA
CPSIA information can be obtained
at www.ICGtesting.com
LVHW042340270724
786707LV00019B/93